Stories for Every Holiday

BY

CAROLYN SHERWIN BAILEY

THE ABINGDON PRESS
NEW YORK   CINCINNATI

Republished by Gale Research Company, Book Tower, Detroit, 1974

Library of Congress Cataloging in Publication Data

Bailey, Carolyn Sherwin, 1875-1961.
    Stories for every holiday.

        SUMMARY: Twenty-seven short stories about twenty
holidays throughout the year.
        Reprint of the 1918 ed.
        1. Holidays--Juvenile fiction. [1. Holidays--Fiction.
2. Short stories] I. Title.
PZ7.B151Ste9   [Fic]   73-20149
ISBN 0-8103-3957-9

CONTENTS

4 CONTENTS

THE NEW BOY

"WHAT are you boys going to do tomorrow?" Tom Fisher asked of the group sitting on the school steps.

"How about taking a lunch and some tackle over to Roaring Brook for a day's fishing?" Bob Tennant suggested. "Father's got a lot of new goods in the store and he might let me have fishhooks for the whole crowd."

"Good for you, Bob," Harold Bascomb said, giving Bob a rousing slap on his back, "but I was thinking we ought to get in a practice game of ball before Labor Day. We'll never lick the Shelton nine with your recent batting, Bob."

Bob's face flushed. "Shelton'll outscore us anyway, Herbert, so what's the use of trying? Look at the fine suits they've got, and the dandy school they come from over in their town—solid brick with a furnace, and a roof that doesn't leak. Nobody expects much of us over here in Brewster. We're like the school—kind of shabby, and we play a shabby game of ball."

Tom Fisher looked up at the weather-stained

walls and eaves of the little Brewster school. It had sheltered and fostered many beginnings of the great in its day; boys who had turned out to be lawyers and statesmen and ministers had carved their names on its desks and gone over its thresholds to write them again in the world's hall of fame. But the schoolhouse looked like a dusty, brown, vagabond sitting and sunning himself beside the road. The big chimney with its loosened bricks might have been the tramp's rimless hat, and the loosened shingles his unkempt fringe of hair. The little windows looked like sleepy eyes, and the weather-stained framework and weedy yard were the ragged garments of this wayside wreck, the Brewster district school.

Tom laughed as he spoke. "Wonder what the new teacher will think of it. He isn't in town yet, and he's a Yale man too. Guess he'll think he's come to some old fossil all right. Father says the selectmen don't want to waste any money on repairs, for they're thinking of putting up a new schoolhouse before long. But whenever they talk about doing it, they decide to put it off because they hate to tear down this old building where they went when they were boys."

"Well, it's our school. It isn't theirs,"

Bob broke in. "Remember the night we initiated scouts down here?"

"And the time we dressed up like Indians and scared the girls at their sewing class, Tom?"

"Scared them not!" Harold said. "They knew all about it when you tipped over your war paint in the barn, Bob, and your sister told."

"Well, we've had a lot of fun in our school," Bob asserted, "and what I was thinking about it was this—" He lowered his voice, although there was no one in sight up or down the road, and he began to unfold a plan to the others. As Bob talked the boys listened with more and more eagerness.

"How did you ever think of it, Bob?"

"Do you suppose we can do it without being found out?"

"We've got a whole week before Labor Day."

"Maybe the new boy will help."

The sentences flashed around the group and fishing and baseball were forgotten in the plan that had found its way into an unexpected place, Bob Tennant's heart.

"Who is the new boy, anyway?" Tom asked now. "I know he's older than we are and is boarding at Mrs. Jennings's, but I don't know his name."

"Nobody seems to know his name," Harold

said. "I suppose he's come to go to school in the upper class. Guess he's a relative of somebody important who graduated from Brewster. We'll find out about him when school opens."

"He comes down to the store almost every afternoon," Bob said. "If I see him, I'll tell him he can come in on the scheme," he finished, getting up and leading the boys out to the road. "Then the fishing's off?" he asked, as they separated to go home.

"Everything's off," Harold decided, "until we finish."

It happened that Bob met the new boy in his father's general store that afternoon. It was difficult to class him, tall and slender as he was, but with a young face. His outing suit was different from Brewster-cut clothes and made him seem young. Yet his eyes were so dark and steady in their gaze that they gave one the impression that he was older. He was at the sport counter trying on some baseball gloves, so Bob accosted him.

"Play ball?" Bob asked.

A boyish smile lighted the stranger's face. "I used to," he replied, noncommitally.

"Going to be in the upper class at Brewster?" Bob continued.

The strange boy looked astonished and did not speak for a moment. Then his face positively beamed. "I hope I'll get in pretty close range of the upper class," he answered.

This was the opening Bob wanted. He spoke in a low tone, explaining his plan. "We ought to be able to finish by Labor Day," he added. "We'll let you in on it," he said, patronizingly.

The stranger gripped Bob's hand. "That's awfully good of you," he said, gratefully. "I don't know anybody here, and I wanted to get acquainted with some of you fellows if I could before school opens. Did you say there was to be a ball game Labor Day afternoon?"

Bob nodded. "Shelton," he explained; "swell suits, good players, coming over to make us score zero."

"But you mustn't let them!" The new boy was all earnestness now. "Haven't you got any pride here in Brewster?"

"We haven't got any suits and we're ashamed of ourselves," Bob said. "Well, good-by; see you to-morrow. O, what's your name?"

"Saunders," the strange boy said, promptly.

"I wonder if it's his last or his first name," Bob thought as the slender figure strolled out of the store; but there was so much to do before the next day that Bob never asked himself the question again.

Every home where there was a boy in Brewster the following day had its surprises, pleasant or otherwise. Tom Fisher refused an invitation to his grandfather's farm to stay until school opened, and explained that he would rather do errands half a day for the grocery store because he wanted to earn some money. Harold, who loved to ride on his father's engine during vacation, gave up the privilege, although he had the opportunity to help the stoker from Brewster to Shelton and back several times. Bob was caught trying to go up the back stairs without being seen, his new corduroy suit decorated with green paint. And he made not the slightest objection to wearing a jumper and overalls for the rest of the week before school began. In fact, he seemed to take the change of garments with unusual cheerfulness.

All of the boys were gone from their homes from breakfast until supper time, and came in dog tired and as hungry as bears.

"Up to some mischief," a few people said.

"O, the boys are all right. They're finishing their vacation with scouting, or digging a cave, or practicing ball," the majority of the fathers and mothers decided. What did surprise them though was the notice posted in the general store the afternoon before Labor Day:

All the citizens of Brewster who are alumni of the Brewster School are invited to come down to the school on the morning of Labor Day. The school will be open for inspection.

Signed,
Tom Fisher
Bob Tennant
Harold Holcomb,
Committee on Repairs.

There was hardly a man or woman in Brewster who had not at one time or another crossed the school's worn doorsill. The old men chuckled at the notice and then had to wipe the mist off their spectacles. The boys' fathers straightened themselves proudly and said, "Nothing like the enterprise of the younger generation, is there?"

No one failed to accept the invitation. The morning of Labor Day saw a crowd of eager pedestrians hurrying down what had come to be called the School House Road. It was headed by Judge Fisher, Tom's grandfather, with his tall hat and gold-headed cane. Bringing up the rear was old Jerry Peters, from the Poor Farm. Everyone was looking for a surprise, but not the one that met them when they reached the schoolhouse and thronged the yard and open doors.

The boys, led by Saunders, had worked fast and secretly. The situation of the school just off the beaten track of the town had also helped. As if the roadside vagabond had suddenly arisen, put on the garments of civilization, and renewed his old pride, so the old schoolhouse was transformed.

The boys had filled in the loose bricks of the chimney with new ones. The roof was reshingled. The schoolhouse was painted. Cracked panes of glass were replaced by unbroken ones, and there were no longer flying blinds, broken hinges, or leaking gutters. The yard was neat, and a new gravel path led from the gate to the front door. The fence shone with a coat of fresh paint and not a picket was missing. A peaceful army of boy laborers armed with paint and brushes, hammers, saws, and nails, and shovels and rakes had worked the miracle. Even the flagpole was painted, and from the top there floated a new flag which Saunders had contributed.

No one knew what to say at first. Everybody crowded into the upper class room at last and squeezed, three and four at a desk, as Judge Fisher stood up in front of them on the platform.

"Speech!" they cried, but before he began the Judge beckoned for Tom, and Bob, and Harold to come and stand beside him.

"We all want to thank these three boys," he said, "for giving us just what we needed on Labor Day—an example of honest work done for the good of the community. We need a new school, but the old one shall always stand as a monument to the industry of our boys. I suggest that we give them three cheers."

But Bob spoke, his eagerness taking away all his shyness:

"It wasn't just us, Judge Fisher. We never could have done it all alone if it hadn't been for the new boy, Saunders. He sent for the paint, and paid for the shingles, and showed us how to lay bricks and set glass. We ought to cheer for Saunders, Judge Fisher. There he is, right over there by the door."

The Judge followed with a glance the direction in which Bob pointed. He looked puzzled and repeated Bob's words to himself.

"The new boy—Saunders?" Then a look of amusement flashed across his face. "Of course," he said, motioning toward the back of the room. "Won't you join us—Professor Saunders?"

The cheers rocked the room. They were

followed by ripples of laughter that broke into waves of merriment as the fathers and mothers enjoyed the blushes and chagrin of the boys, who looked in amazed surprise at their new teacher.

The new boy who had bossed their gang for the jolly work on the schoolhouse, who had seemed not so much older than they, and who had been their good pal was the Yale man come down to take charge of the Brewster school!

But Professor Saunders met the situation with the same skill with which he had mixed mortar and laid bricks. He threw a kind arm about Bob's shoulders.

"It was a little subterfuge on my part, coming here unannounced," he said. "I wanted to get acquainted with the Brewster boys before school began. I'm not much beyond boyhood myself, and I wanted to begin my work here by helping the boys to feel how much I like everything that they do. But I never should have been able to carry out my plan if Bob hadn't let me have a share in his. Painting and shingling a schoolhouse together is a fine way of getting ready to work together in it.

"It gave me an idea too," he continued. "We're going to make a record for scholarship in our school this year to keep pace with the work we did on the outside. We've put a uniform on the schoolhouse, speaking figuratively. A uniform helps," he stepped behind the desk on the platform and pulled out a big package.

"Open it, boys?" he said.

The three pulled off the wrappings and took out gray shirts with big B's in red on the front, baseball caps and trousers.

"Suits for this afternoon's game!" they exclaimed delightedly.

"And for making Shelton's score zero," Professor Saunders said. "We'll work in our diamond as well as we worked on the schoolhouse. Out of school, I'm Saunders of Yale, remember that, boys."

HOW THEY KEPT LABOR DAY

"I'VE thought of a splendid plan for Labor Day, girls!" Madeliene dropped down on the grass of Helen Maynard's lawn, her eyes shining with eagerness. The other girls, a half dozen or so, were grouped about in the hammock, in chairs, or on the grass talking over the vacation and the coming holiday that was always celebrated by the little town of Mill River. A thriving mill and a factory on the edge of the river, and several flourishing business blocks helped to make the town's prosperity. Labor Day would begin with flying flags. It would go on through a morning's parade, speaking, and a band concert in the park in the afternoon and fireworks in the evening. Industry and honest work had made Mill River the pleasant place to live in that it was, and the town believed in keeping the holiday fittingly. Even the girls were planning to have a share in it.

"What, Madeliene?" The other girls were all excitement too.

Madeliene Bridgman's mother was the town dressmaker, and Madeliene had splendid ideas, always, about pageants or the school dramatics.

16

In her clever hands a few yards of cheese-cloth and a roll of tinsel could be transformed into a robe for Titania.

Madeliene got up now and unfolded her scheme.

"Your father is master of ceremonies on Labor Day, Helen," she began. "I thought that perhaps he would let us girls march in the parade, and we can dress up to represent women characters who stand for work. I can be Minerva," she said, "the goddess of all the weavers. I thought of that on account of mother's working so much with cloth. Minerva was a character in Greek mythology, so all I shall need will be a Grecian tunic, quite long, and a band around my hair, and I can carry a small weaving frame. Mother will make my dress so I shall not have to bother about it," she finished.

"O, how splendid!" Helen said. "I know father will say that we may march. I know what I shall be, Friga, the Norse goddess of the home. My hair is as long and as fair as hers is in the pictures, and my dress can be long and trimmed with cotton batting for ermine. I shall wear a gold crown and carry a torch to signify the lighted hearths of the homes all over the earth. Mother was going over to Feeding Hills to visit grandmother for the day, but I know she will stay at home so I can celebrate Labor Day," Helen said, decidedly.

The two girl friends, Madeliene and Helen, had given the others their cue.

"I shall be Ceres," Muriel said. "Everybody is thinking of the harvest now, and mother is doing up the fruits and vegetables at our house. She is making tomato catsup and peach preserves and plum jam. Ceres was the goddess of the harvest, and I can wear a Greek costume like Madeliene's and carry a big cardboard horn of plenty full of fruits."

"I am going to be Justice and carry scales," Elizabeth, the town lawyer's little daughter, announced.

"And I shall dress as a Red Cross nurse," said one.

"And I as a teacher in cap and gown," decided another.

"All we need in the way of material for the costumes is plenty of cheap white and black cambric," Madeliene said. She had appointed herself a committee of one on ways and means as usual, and the others willingly followed her lead. "Anything in the way of headdresses or things to carry that we need can be made of cardboard, covered with colored paper, or we can paint them. We'll meet at my

house to sew and we've got all of a week in
which to get ready. O, where's Janet, though?"
she asked, looking over the group.

As if in answer to her question there was a
click of the gate and the girls heard a clear
trilling call like a bird's. There were flying
steps on the gravel path and a girl in Camp
Fire dress and moccasins, her long brown
braids hanging below her waist, stood among
them.

"Janet! O, we have the best ever plan for
Labor Day." The girls crowded about the
newcomer explaining. Janet listened, her
cheeks rosy with pleasure and her brown
eyes darker than before.

"You can be the spirit of the Camp Fire
Girls, Janet—honors earned by work," Helen
said. "All you will need will be your Camp
Fire dress," she added, kindly, to try and
set Janet at ease as regarded her costume.
There was no home in all Mill River so merry
as Janet Travers's little gray one down by
the factory. Such candy-pulls and story hours
and fireside games as its low roof had sheltered! Yet Janet was the girl in their class
at school who had the least of the world's
comforts and the most responsibility. Her
father had been killed in the factory, and she
was the oldest, at thirteen, of a big brood in

the little gray nest. As Helen spoke, the light and color faded slowly from Janet's face.

"I just wish I could be in the fun with you all," she sighed, "but I guess I'll have to keep on being the spirit of the Camp Fire at home. It seems as if everything that could happen to us has happened this summer. Jimmy's got the whooping cough and the baby's coming down with it. You know mother and I have papered the whole house and painted the woodwork this summer, and mother's so tired she'll never be able to take the position as forewoman in the factory they've offered her if she can't go away for a little rest first. We've saved enough for her to have a whole week in the country, with lots of milk and eggs, and she's going to-day. I just ran over to see you a minute before she starts. I shall be busy at home all the rest of the time until school opens."

"O, Janet; it's too bad!"

"We did want you so!"

The girls' sympathy was real. They put their arms around the little girl of Camp Fire honors and tried to persuade her to join them, even at the last minute, but she was firm. She turned and left them and they watched her slim brown figure going swiftly down the

street until she was lost to them between the
lines of shade trees.

The following days were full of fun and
sewing for the girls.   Madeliene's mother
found her dressmaking delayed as the girls
called upon her for pins, needles, ideas as to
color schemes, and help in fitting.   It meant
evenings of picking up dropped stitches for
her, but the girls' costumes grew in a fasci-
nating fashion in her sewing room.   The long
Greek robes hung in graceful lines and were
decorated with borders of yellow cambric
cut in a Grecian design and sewed on.   Friga's
northern dress was designed and also a red
cloak.   Ceres's dress was trimmed with bunches
of real wheat, and a college cloak and mortar-
board of black cambric were soon ready for
the girl who was to represent the teaching
profession.

"You are going to sit up late again this
evening, mother?"   Madeliene asked a few
nights before Labor Day as she saw her mother
bent over the sewing machine in the gas light.

"I don't see how I shall finish these orders
if I don't," her mother replied.   "Good night,
dear.   Pleasant dreams!"

It was Madeliene's imagination, of course,
but as she went upstairs her bedroom candle
seemed to cast a shadow on the wall of a

little Camp Fire girl watching beside the crib
of a sick baby.

Helen spent so much time at Madeliene's,
working on her dress, that when she did see
her father she forgot to ask him whether or
not the girls might have a division in the
Labor Day parade. She had found a book
on Norse mythology at the library and was
so interested reading the legends about Friga,
the character whom she was to represent,
that she found very little opportunity, either,
to help her mother with the fall house-cleaning.

"You aren't going to grandmother's, are you,
on Labor Day?" she asked one afternoon.
"We girls are going to have a kind of pageant
and I am to be the goddess of the home in it.
I'm going down to Madeliene's now to sew on
my cloak."

Mrs. Maynard looked down from the step
ladder on which she was cleaning windows.

"I wish you would stop on your way and
send up six more cakes of soap, Helen," she
said. "No, I don't expect to get away on
Labor Day," she added. "I shall not have
finished the cleaning."

Helen passed Janet's house on her way to
the grocery store. Sleeves rolled up and her
arms white with soap suds, Janet was washing
in the open kitchen door. She waved a wet

hand to Helen. She was laughing, but Helen's face grew sober as she went on to Madeliene's.

"Janet's really keeping house," she thought, suddenly, "and I'm only dressing up, to look like somebody in a story who believed in being a homemaker."

The day before Labor Day, Muriel, who was to be Ceres, went into the kitchen to select some fruits and vegetables for her horn of plenty. Her mother, bent low over a pan of tomatoes, looked up and motioned toward the pantry. Her face was flushed with the heat from the big preserving kettle whose savory contents simmered on the stove, and her fingers were cracked and stained.

"I should think something bright like carrots, and apples and a squash would be pretty, Muriel," she said. "There ought to be a bunch of grapes in the top of the horn of plenty too. Won't you pick them out yourself, dear. I can't leave my work. I don't expect to even see the parade to-morrow; it takes so long to get tomatoes ready for canning, and these must be done up at once or they will spoil," she ended with a kind of worried note in her voice.

Muriel did as her mother had suggested, but as she finished and laid the purple grapes on top of the beautiful horn of plenty, she saw Janet hurrying by. She had her market basket, filled, on her arm. It was strange, but Muriel looked with less pleasure at her own symbol of the harvest, seeing Janet carrying home the same fruits with which to feed her small brothers and sisters.

The morning of Labor Day was gloriously bright. Helen, half smiles and half tears, waited on the lawn for the other girls. The smiles were for her mother, who had just left for the visit to Feeding Hills.

"I'm going to be Friga, really, mother, and not just by dressing up," Helen had said as she went to work to help with the house cleaning. "You can go to grandmother's if we finish in time, can't you?" she had asked.

So the house was as fresh as the bright September morning and Helen was left in charge for the day. Seeing her mother's happiness was almost equal to wearing Friga's royal red robes, Helen thought as she waited, dressed in a linen skirt and smock. Hot tears would make their scalding way down her cheeks, though, as she remembered her father's words of the evening before when she had at last remembered to ask him if the girls might march in the parade.

"Of course not, my dear. The different divisions of the parade were all arranged weeks ago. I'm sorry, Helen, but you should have asked me earlier." His words repeated themselves again and again.

How should she tell the girls? Helen wondered. They were to meet at her house, dress, and then start. It was late; they should be there now. The echoes of the band came flaring up the street. Helen went to the gate and looked up and down. Not a girl was in sight.

"I wonder what is making them so late," Helen asked herself. "And, O, I wonder what they will say to me when I tell them they can't march," she thought. "But it's getting long past ten o'clock and the parade starts at ten."

It was near noon when Madeliene came. She wore a gingham dress and had not even brought her Minerva costume.

"Where are the rest?" she asked, wonderingly. "It's all right about our not marching. Don't blame yourself one bit, Helen. I was not going to anyway. I've been helping mother to finish some orders."

Muriel came a few moments later. Her white hands were dark with fruit stains, but she had a shining face, she was so happy.

"I emptied my horn of plenty into the preserving kettle," she said. "Don't look so surprised, girls. I mean that I've been helping mother do up tomatoes at home. She needed me. I suppose you had a beautiful time in the parade," she said, longingly.

"We didn't go," Helen and Madeliene said together.

"I told the others how I felt about it," Madeliene said. "I guess most all of us have been keeping Labor Day at home," Helen laughed.

"Just like Janet," Muriel said. Then, as she looked up the street, she spoke to Helen. "There's a messenger boy coming. I believe he's on his way here."

The messenger stopped at the Maynards' gate. Helen broke the seal of the note he gave her.

"It's from father!" she shouted. "Listen, girls!" She read the letter:

We were all so sorry that we couldn't have our patriotic little daughters in the parade this morning. I am writing from the office, for I am too busy to come home for dinner, but if you and the other girls want to dress up in your costumes and come down to the office after supper, I will see that you have a good place to look at the fireworks. You can stand on one of the floats and be a kind of tableau if you like, with colored lights, so we can all see you.

FATHER.

"O, it's going to come true after all!" Helen said, happily. "And it will be down by the river near Janet's," she added.

The same kind thought had come to all three at the same time.

"We can go down late this afternoon and help her get supper and do the dishes and put all the *whooping-coughers* to sleep," Muriel said.

"She can be with us on the float," Madeliene added.

"I believe it all happened just so she could," Helen finished, "for she knew in the very first place the best way to celebrate Labor Day."

THE DISCOVERERS

"' **A**LL dressed up and no place to go.' "
Ted Blake heard again, in imagination, his little sister's laughing comment as he had started out right after breakfast on the morning of Columbus Day, dressed in his Scout uniform.

"I guess Lucy was about right," Ted said to himself. "It doesn't seem like any other holiday because there's so little a fellow can do. Columbus took a long trip and did a great deed when he discovered the islands off America. We ought to celebrate the day America first became ours, but how can we do it?"

"Out for an adventure, Ted?"

The boy looked up to see Mr. Penfield, his Scout master, just turning the corner and coming toward him. It was almost as if he had read Ted's thoughts. "You're all dressed for one," Mr. Penfield went on, "and Columbus Day is just the day for a Boy Scout to celebrate."

"But I don't know how to," the boy said, hat in hand, as he faced his leader. "There's no new place to go anywhere in or around this little old town of Medford, and not a thing about it that we boys didn't discover long ago."

Mr. Penfield smiled. "If Christopher Columbus had felt that way, he probably wouldn't have had his great adventure. The whole world, as he knew it, told him that there was nothing new to find, but he sailed away with the firm belief that there is always something new somewhere. Go out and discover, my boy." Mr. Penfield took Ted's hand, and turned to go on to his office. "A discovery is hidden, you know. You have to look for it," he added. Ted squared his shoulders and swung down the street. He didn't quite see how one could emulate the great Columbus in Medford, but somehow he felt inspired. He left the town's main street and walked along toward the park. Just at the edge of the park, where a row of thick pine trees grew, and gave the effect of the border of a forest, he saw a flash of color. He pushed in through the trees and then began to laugh.

The girl of about his own age, who started to go on and then stopped, looked at him questioningly.

"I don't see what you're laughing at, Ted," she said. "I just came down here to play, all by myself, that I was an Indian alone in

an American forest. I thought it was about
the only way I could keep Columbus Day."

Ted sobered in a minute, and looked appre-
ciatively at Janet Penfield's Camp Fire dress,
beaded moccasins, and the bead band that
confined her hair. She made a picture, with
the pines for a background and the warm
October sun lighting her bright face, that
quite suited the day.

"I wasn't laughing at you, Janet—honor
bright I wasn't," he assured his friend. "I
was thinking of what your father just said
to me about making discoveries right here in
Medford if I only looked for them, and here
the very first thing I do is to find an American
Indian."

Janet laughed too now. "That would be
fun, wouldn't it?" she went on, "if we could
discover things. Let's go farther on in the
picnic grove here, and see what we can
find."

"All right, let's," Ted assented as he followed his Camp Fire neighbor on between the
trees.

"Look at it; isn't that just a shame," Janet
said at last as they came to the space in the
center of the grove where there had been a
picnic the Saturday before. The rustic seats
and tables were covered with fruit skins and

bits of food; papers and empty boxes littered the ground.

"Discovery number two," Ted said, "but not so pleasant as the first one. Let's try and clean up the grove. The Park Department put new tin cans here the first of the summer for rubbish; it's a pity the kids can't use them."

The two went to work at once. Janet made a broom of twigs and brushed off the tables into the boxes that Ted held for her. The boy picked up the scattered papers from the carpet of pine needles, and put them in the rubbish cans. They worked industriously until the grove was put in order once more.

"Now it's pretty again," Janet said at last with a sigh of satisfaction. "It looks like a new place."

"That's just it—new," Ted exclaimed. "You've given me an idea, Janet. I'm going to get the Scouts together and see if we can't make some more Columbus Day discoveries of old places that need to be made new."

"And I'll get some of the girls," Janet added, enthusiastically. "We'll go out for a Columbus Day adventure too!"

They started out of the park and ran, side by side, through the streets where their boy and girl friends lived, calling at their houses, and telling them of their holiday fun.

In less than an hour there was quite a party of Boy Scouts and Camp Fire girls under the leadership of Ted and Janet.

"We'll go out in small groups," Ted said, "and see what we can discover that needs looking after in our neighborhoods.

"Then we'll meet at our house and report late this afternoon," Janet surprised them all by deciding. She had slipped into her father's office for a few moments when Ted was not looking and had come out with shining eyes and an air of mystery.

"All right, Janet," Ted assented. "Well, then, we're off."

They had never known how full of discoveries their familiar home town of Medford was, or how much there was that they could do to make it a better town. The Boy Scouts found an alley that needed cleaning.

"The kids in those tenements will get sick," Ted said, "with all this dirt right under their windows."

So the boys went to work with brooms and shovels and transformed the alley into a place of neatness in no time.

They found a smoldering bonfire in a side street, perilously near a board fence, and threw water on it. They discovered that the school playground needed cleaning. The school garden looked very much in need of attention, and so they took out the old vines and dead bushes. Wherever they found papers blown through the street by the fall wind, they collected them. They raked up leaves, and cleaned their own home yards and paths.

The Camp Fire girls were quite as busy. They met the town librarian on her way down to the library as they started out, and flocked about her, telling of their plan. "Please come with us, Miss Ferguson," they begged.

"O, I can't do that; it isn't a holiday for me, you know," the librarian replied. "I am going to have an especially busy day too, for I want to get the shelves of children's books in order. And I am going to put all the stories of American discoveries and inventions together so that you and the boys can read this week about what America has accomplished since 1492."

"O, could we help you put those books together on our shelves?" Janet asked.

"Why, yes," Miss Ferguson said. "That would be a great help."

It seemed to the girls as they discovered books about the wonders of the telegraph, the steam engine, the telephone, the cable, and the automobile, that they were real Indians, following with the years the trail of American progress. The stories looked more wonderful than fairy tales, and as they put the books out on a special shelf under the picture of the landing of Columbus, they thought of the surprise they would be to their friends, the Boy Scouts. Then they searched the town gardens for late blossoms, the hardy orange marigolds and bright dahlias, and filled some jars with these and bright leaves to make the library beautiful.

Miss Ferguson gave a sigh of relief as she looked about at this work. "Well, this is a discovery for me," she said when the girls told her good-by. "You girls have made this old town library look like new. Thank you so much."

"Wohelo! Work, health, love!" Janet said as the Camp Fire girls stood together in the square outside of the library. "I wonder what else we can do to make our watchword come true."

"Let's go home now," suggested one of the girls, "and see what we can find there that needs to be done. We can make some attic and kitchen and backyard discoveries, I am quite sure," she said with a wry face, "and make things look different. We can play that our homes are our wigwams and we are getting them ready to welcome Columbus."

"O, yes," Janet said, "and then meet at my house at four o'clock."

They were tired but cheerful Scouts and Camp Fire girls who gathered on the Penfield piazza late in the afternoon. They were surprised, though, to find hampers packed with mysteriously bulging packages and Mr. and Mrs. Penfield waiting for them, dressed for a hike.

"We're going to take the street car to Bear Ridge, and then go along the trail and climb the mountain for a real Indian camp fire and supper," Janet explained to Ted. And when Ted told the others, three cheers of delight rang out through the crisp fall air. The boys took the baskets and the girls, carrying paper plates, cups and napkins, led the merry way.

It was a short trip on the car, and Bear Ridge was not much more than a wooded hill, but when the boys and girls saw the first bright rays of the sunset touching its top as they climbed it, they felt like explorers coming upon a new land. The boys built a rousing fire in a clearing as the girls unpacked the ears of roasting corn, little sausages, potatoes, bread and butter sandwiches and old-fashioned pickles that the hampers had hidden.

"We must plant our standard," Mr. Penfield

said as he unrolled the Stars and Stripes he had
brought with him and placed the flag in the
ground at the edge of the clearing. The Scouts
gathered about it and saluted the colors, and
then sang "America." All about them were
trees and rocks, but below, in the valley, they
could see the smoke rising from the Medford
chimneys.

"It's just as if we were really Columbus and
his party landing in America!" Janet exclaimed
as the last notes of the singing died away.

"And you can keep on being discoverers all
the year," her father said. "You can look for
new things to do that will help our town, and
new places to fly our colors because of your
service to others," he said. The boys and
girls were quiet a moment, listening to and
remembering the Scout master's words. Then
they circled the camp fire, and supper began.

There were surely never such sweet ears
of corn, such mealy potatoes, or toothsome
sausages. The boys cut pointed sticks to use
for the roasting, and everybody ate as if they
were starved. After the substantial part of
the feast was over, Mrs. Penfield brought out
another surprise, a box of marshmallows to
toast over the glowing coals. And as the boys
and girls sat about in the glow of the fire
Mrs. Penfield read aloud to them the story of

the intrepid discoverer whose holiday they were keeping.

As the sun faded and there was little light except that of the embers the boys and girls sang together again, then covered the ashes and started down the trail toward home. But everything seemed, in some unusual way, different and better to them than it had in the morning. It had been a day of finding out how splendid and new things were, and Ted, leading the way with Janet, expressed the feelings of them all as he said, "Columbus Day is one of the best days of all, isn't it?"

HALLOWEEN IN PRECINCT B

TERRY pulled himself up on to the captain's stool and put his elbows on the desk. His legs swung a long way from the worn floor of the station house. His merry face twinkled with smiles like that of some elf as he looked across the piles of ledgers and over at the old man in the corner.

"It's Halloween, Maguire!" he said.

"Sure and don't I know that?" the old Irish janitor said, getting up and pouring more coal from the scuttle into the stove. "Don't I remember All-Hallow Eve in the old country when I was a boy—everybody out listening for the fairies, and watching for ghosts on the churchyard wall. Then the games in the barns, and plenty of apples and cakes! All-Hallow Eve's a fine time, lad. Nobody knows it better than Patrick Maguire."

"Well, it seems like Halloween here in the city a bit, anyway," Terry said cheerfully, pointing to the window that looked out on the street. "I went over to Jasmine's father's store this afternoon and, O, such fat pumpkins as she was selling, and red apples, and bags of nuts! I tried to tell Jasmine about Hal-

38

loween, but she's an East Indian girl and couldn't understand how we keep it up.

" 'What does Halloween really mean, little master of the precinct?' she asked. 'O, Jack-o'-Lanterns, and spiders, and witches, and snakes!' I said. Then her eyes got so big. 'Not snakes!' she said. 'O, yes,' I told her, and she seemed so surprised. Girls are all 'fraid-cats, aren't they, Maguire? "

"I don't know about that," Maguire said, thoughtfully. "I've known girls in Ireland every bit as plucky as a boy. But Terry, lad, do you know the real meaning of the Eve?"

Terry got down from his stool and went over beside the old man.

"Why, no, Maguire," he said. "What does Halloween really mean?"

The old Irishman took off the cap he had been wearing, and lowered his voice. "It's the night when we keep in mind the folks we love who've gone to heaven. That's how it began and that's how it ought to end, Terry."

"Father!" the boy breathed, softly.

"Faith, yes!" Maguire echoed. "The finest, bravest policeman that ever lost his life in doing his duty in the precinct. Where would this station have been, or the children in the tenements that night if he hadn't carried out the box of powder that was half lighted when he found it? That's why you're the mascot of Precinct B, lad, because we were so proud of your father. Never forget him, lad."

Terry's eyes filled with tears that he couldn't keep back.

"I think of father day and night, Maguire. Mother'll tell you how I try to make up to her for him, and I'm proud of being the mascot here." He touched his big tin badge that the force had given him. "If there's ever anything I can do to help, you know I'll do it."

"Sure, we do, lad," Maguire said, patting Terry's back. "And there's something now. I'm hungry as a pig for my tea and potatoes, and the captain's not due to be back for a half hour yet. Could you mind the station, laddie, for that, and answer the phone, and send out a call, if it's needed, to headquarters? It's bound to be quiet. Everybody's having a good time, not thinking about doing harm."

"Could I, Maguire? O, just try me!" Terry said.

"All right. I might be back any minute, and you'll have the captain himself before you know it." Maguire lighted his pipe, pulled on his cap, and went out into the crisp night air.

Through the opened door there came the shrill singing of the chestnuts roasting out-

side. A boy passed by waving a grotesque
false face. Terry peered out. Then he closed
the door and stood in the middle of the room.
There wasn't a prouder boy in the whole city
than he.

"Maybe I can't make a Jack-o'-Lantern
or bob for apples this Halloween," he said,
"but I can take father's place. O, I do wish
something would happen!"

As if in answer to his wish, the door of the
station house opened noiselessly and then
closed. Terry turned to see a large tin box
that had been shoved in by some strange hand.
There were a few small holes perforated in
the top and it fastened in an old-fashioned
way by means of a pin thrust in a hasp.

Terry ran to the window and looked out.
No one was to be seen either up or down the
street. Whoever had brought in the mysterious
box had made his escape. Terry went on tiptoe
over to it and saw for the first time that there
was a folded piece of paper stuck in the hasp.
He carefully pulled it out and unfolded it.
The writing was in an awkward, crooked hand,
but it was plain enough.

Terry crept behind the big desk, his heart
beating so loudly that he could scarcely hear
the ticking of the big wall clock. At seven
the captain and the day shift would be in and

the night shift ready to go out. Every policeman in the precinct would come, and perhaps
the box was something that could do them
harm. Terry loved every one of the husky,
good-natured, heroic bluecoats. So did everybody on the beat. Didn't they help the
school children to cross the crowded streets,
and look after the lost cats and dogs of the
neighborhood, and have a Christmas tree in
the station house with a gift for every child?
These thoughts flashed through Terry's mind.
He must open the box, now, he thought and
save his policeman friends. But as he stepped
toward it, the box moved slightly. Terry
jumped. He felt cold and covered with goose
flesh. After all, he was only a boy of eleven,
and alone.

"I can't touch it. I don't dare," he said.
It seemed now as if his heart had stopped
beating altogether and he heard the clock.
It was striking a quarter before seven. With
the sound, Maguire's words about his father
came back to Terry.

"The finest, bravest policeman that ever
lost his life in doing his duty—"

That decided Terry. Nothing mattered now
save that he must do his duty in the precinct,
trying to take his father's place. He went
bravely up to the box, kneeled on the floor,

and took the pin out of the hasp. He pulled
the hasp.

Just then he heard a sound of merry whistling
in the street outside. It came nearer. Maguire,
happy after his supper, was coming back to
the station house whistling "The Wearing of
the Green." Nobody in the precinct had a
way of whistling like the old Irishman. It
beat the pipes any day.

Terry gasped, lifted the cover of the mysterious box, and fell back, white and amazed,
just as Maguire came in the door, still whistling
loudly. As the lid of the box lifted, the head
of a huge green snake appeared, followed by
its lithe, twisting body. It looked out, its
jewel-like eyes flashing in the dim light. Then
it began to sway its head and neck gracefully
in time to Maguire's music. It was uncanny.
The snake was dancing.

Maguire's terror brought Terry to his feet
and over to the old man's side. Maguire
was shaking from head to foot as he pointed
to the snake which had dropped back into
the box again and only peered out now that
the music had stopped.

"The ghost of Saint Patrick; I called him
by my tune!" Maguire moaned, but Terry
held his arm and pointed to the snake.

"Well, don't worry about it anyway, Maguire.

I guess whoever he is, he's tame. I—" but
Terry was interrupted by a little girl bursting
in the door like a breath of wind, bringing the
colors of leaves and the perfume of the harvest
in its trail. Her dark hair was held back by
a crimson turban. She wore a shawl of woven
orange and yellow, and beneath her embroidered dress were strangely fashioned, Oriental
slippers. She had an accordeon in her hand.

"Jasmine!" Terry exclaimed.

The little girl stamped her foot and pointed
to the clock.

"I said to wait until seven. Then I would
come when the store was closed and play for
our Alonzo to dance. He is one of the best-
trained snakes of the East. My father was
a snake-charmer there, but here one cannot
earn enough money with dancing snakes, so
we have a store. But we could not part with
Alonzo. He lives in our yard. Here he is!
You said you needed a snake to-night?" she
said, questioningly.

The station house had begun to fill with
policemen now. The captain had taken his
place behind his desk. At Jasmine's words a
laugh filled the room that made Alonzo lift
his head and look about in surprise.

"Play for him, little snake-charmer!"

"We're keeping Halloween all right."

Everyone in the station watched as Jasmine opened and closed her accordeon and Alonzo bent and swayed in perfect time to the rhythm.

Once, as Jasmine stopped, the captain spoke: "Who opened that box? It must have taken some pluck."

There was a moment's silence and then Maguire answered: "The little fellow opened it," he said.

"I thought about father," Terry explained, quickly. "It said on it, *'Wait until seven o'clock'* —just when the men would be coming in off the beat. I didn't want anything to happen to them, if there was something dangerous in it."

In the hush that followed, the men in the room looked at each other and at the boy. But it was Maguire who spoke:

"All-Hallow Eve in Precinct B!" he said.

THE JUNIOR HOME GUARD

IT was most exciting to live near the polling place. Lee and Lucy thought that they had never in all their lives seen anything so interesting as what went on inside the big empty office floor that had been taken over by the town for Election Day.

The two, brother and sister of twelve and eleven, lived at the other end of the block from the polls. From their front gate they could see the preparations for voting that went on for a week before. A great American flag was hung over the door. Small wooden booths were built in the big empty room. A policeman was stationed at the door. His rain coat buttoned up to his ears, he paced back and forth in front of the polling place, although rain soaked his boots, and an early sleet storm cut him in the face.

Lucy sighed as she watched the crowds that gathered to watch everything that was going on near the polls.

"O, I wish I were a boy and could do something for our town some day," she said.

"Well, I wish I were old enough now to vote," Lee added.

One day the children ventured to speak to the policeman.

"They're going to choose a mayor, are they not?" Lee asked.

"He'll be a kind of king, won't he, sitting in the town hall?" Lucy added.

The policeman looked down at the two eager, upturned faces and smiled.

"Bless your hearts," he laughed, "the mayor of this town doesn't do much sitting still. He has to be up and about, seeing that our town is kept clean and fine to live in. He has to look after the Board of Health, and the Fire Department, and the Street Cleaners, and the Home Guard. You see, a very important part of town government is just keeping the town a safe place for boys and girls to grow up in," he finished as he resumed his pacing.

Lee and Lucy looked at each other with wide open eyes as they went home.

"Street Cleaners, and the Home Guards!" Lucy repeated, remembering the policeman's amazing words.

"The town has to be kept a safe place to live in," Lee echoed.

They thought about this army of town workers all the rest of the week; in the lamplight, after supper, and out in their own delightful room of the garage where both could tinker and play to their hearts' delight, and entertain their boy and girl friends in any number. Perhaps it was the excitement of being so near a polling place; perhaps it was the inspiration of seeing the Stars and Stripes flying in front of it; however it came about, though, it was a splendid plan that Lee and Lucy made.

They kept it a secret until they had their garage playroom ready, which wasn't easy, for the neighboring children almost stormed the doors to find out about it. First, Lee cleaned the room. When he told the secret to his father one night, he got Lee an Uncle Sam poster to hang up in the garage. It was wonderfully large and fine to have. They hung a flag over the picture, and Lee made a desk by putting two wooden boxes side by side. Lucy covered the top with red blotting paper, and brought out a pad of white paper and a bottle of blue ink from the home library. She busied herself making a quantity of white cambric badges, bordered at the top with red and at the bottom with blue. Lee lettered all these badges "J. H. G." Their last work was to hang out a big sign over the garage door. It said:

"The Junior Home Guard"

"I wonder if anybody will join," Lucy said, doubtfully, as she took her place on the morning of election day behind the improvised desk.

"There they come now, to find out about it, anyway," Lee said from his place at her side.

Indeed, their friends almost stampeded the junior recruiting station.

"What's it for?"

"May we belong?"

"What do we have to do?"

They fairly shouted the questions, but Lee and Lucy were ready for them. Lucy took charge of the girls and Lee enrolled the boys. Each one put down his or her name on a sheet of paper, their home address, and then the branch of this town army to which they could best belong. The badges were marked:

Engineer Corps.

Canteen Division.

Messenger Service.

And Lucy had insisted upon having a fourth badge labeled Mending Brigade. She was most mysterious about this last division of their army; she did not tell even Lee what it meant.

A great many of the boys enlisted in the Engineer Corps. Those who had roller coasters, roller skates, or bicycles were eligible for the Messenger Service. Most of the girls joined the Canteen Division, but Lucy headed the Mending Brigade, and when she told the girls about it they joined her in large numbers.

Each child received a badge as soon as he or she enlisted.

It was almost supper time before the tired-out recruiting agents had finished, but it had been a good day and a great deal of fun in spite of the hard work.

"They are so excited over it, Lee," Lucy said. "Regular army work begins to-morrow. We'll meet at our Home Guard station and start right out after school."

"Nobody's going to tell," Lee said. "Won't the town be surprised?"

And Lee was right; the town was very much surprised.

There was an early snowfall the following week. Old Mrs. Hastings looked out of her window and wondered how she would ever be able to get across the street to Mr. Billings's grocery shop. At the same moment two of the Engineer Corps, Tom and Billy Alton, arrived on the scene armed with snow shovels. They wore their badges, and they shoveled snow harder and faster than they ever had before, for they were doing it in a new way now. They were part of the Junior Home Guard, keeping the streets safe. It was play as well as work. All over the town the Junior Guards worked, clearing the streets, helping the street cleaners, and gathering up the rubbish.

The town kitchens were invaded by the members of the new Junior Canteen. Wherever there was a little girl with a Canteen badge, pots and pans played tunes, and dishwater glistened with rainbow-tinted soapsuds. The girls put into practice at home the simple cooking that they learned in school. They brought samples of their paper-thin vegetable parings to the Home Guard station to see who wasted the least. They appointed a Canteen Division to be on duty every day in the school lunch room to be sure that no food was thrown away.

About the time of the thaw that followed the snowstorm there was a call for more men for the army. Mr. Billings lost two clerks and three delivery boys; there was the same lack of help in a good many other stores, and that brought the chance for which the Junior Messenger Service had been waiting. When the stores opened on Saturday morning there were two or three of the Junior Messengers, on wheels, waiting at the doors to volunteer their help as package carriers. They were a great help, and they volunteered also for other days after school.

Those of the boys and girls who dropped into the Junior Home Guard station for a brief furlough occasionally found the Mending Brigade busy and cheerful around the little wood stove that heated it.

"We ought to have called ourselves the Daughters of Betsy Ross," Lucy said. "It looks exactly like a flag shop here," she exclaimed. "You see, our flags have been hung out in all kinds of weather so long that a good many of them were beginning to look as if they had been through a war," she explained to the others. "We brought as many as we could here to fix them. And just see how well we are getting on."

It was really wonderful what the Mending Brigade was accomplishing. Torn flags were being carefully stitched into whole ones again. Faded red stripes were being replaced by fresh, new ones. Dingy stars were being covered with clean, white cloth, and Old Glory was appearing, not old, but new in the clever fingers of the little girls who loved the American flag too much to want to see it look tattered.

But there were days when the courage of the Junior Guards almost gave out. It had been play at first, but it meant effort to keep the work of their town army up to the standard they had set. Skating parties, candy pulls, and games had to be given up, but the boys and girls kept on.

"We've enlisted, and that means that nobody can desert," Lee said; and they all realized that this was quite true.

"I'm going to punch holes in these en-rollment papers, Lee, and tie them together with red white, and blue ribbon so that they won't get scattered." Lucy said one day. Then her face grew white. "They're gone!" she said. It was true. Some one had taken the records of the Junior Guard.

They looked for the papers without success for several days, and then one morning they found them quite as mysteriously returned. All the children said they had not touched them. There seemed no way to explain their disappearance, and it worried Lee and Lucy a great deal, until their attention was turned by the announcement of a special assembly in school.

"I wonder what it's for," Lee said.

"To give out more tests I suppose," Lucy replied in a discouraged tone of voice.

But the assembly had been called for a very different reason. When the classes marched, to the music of "Columbia" played by the school band, into the big flag-decked audience room, they saw a visitor in blue, waiting for them on the platform. It was Lee's and Lucy's Election Day policeman.

"I was a boy myself not so long ago," he began

after the children had seated themselves. "That's why I've been so interested to see the boys and girls playing Junior Guard in this town. I like to watch the little station they've been running at the other end of the block from where our polling place was. They're as ship-shape in their way as we were in our office. Once when I was off duty I looked inside it, and asked the lady of the house if I could take their records for a while so as to copy off the names of these plucky little town workers. She said I might, and I slipped the records back, and gave the names to my friend, the principal of this school. He told the mothers and fathers about the Junior Guards, and they've planned a surprise for the boys and girls. That's all I have to say, except that I want to shake hands with my fellow officers who did the planning. And now, three cheers for our town!"

They gave them; and it was repeated three times three. Then came the surprise. The name of each Junior Home Guard was called, and they went up to the platform to receive their gifts from the mothers and fathers; red, white, and blue middy ties for the girls, and enameled flag buttons for the boys. As each Junior Guard went up the whole school applauded. When Lee and Lucy went up and shook hands with the policeman, and then stood for a moment, one on each side of him, it seemed as if the school would never stop clapping.

It was the best thing that the children had done all that winter, everybody said; and it turned out to last longer than Lee and Lucy had ever thought it would. They discovered that there was something for a Junior Guard to do every day in the year in his town, and a good deal of fun in doing it too.

TURNING THE THANKSGIVING TABLES

NONE of the scholars in the Blake School liked to have the orphans attend it.

The arrangement by which the long line of "all-alone" boys and girls in their "all-alike" blue suits and long blue dresses took their way every morning from the Orphans' Home and came to the brick school building had only been made that fall. Chester was a comfortable little town, its tree-lined streets stretching lazily along until they ended in fertile fields and farm lands outside the village limits. Almost everyone owned a home, and the children did not know what it meant to be poor and an orphan. They somehow resented the fact that the big white Orphans' Home was a part of Chester.

"They ought to live out in the country somewhere," Dorothy Turner, the history teacher's little daughter, said, as she moved away from the school gate to let the orphans in one morning in November. "I'm sure they would be happier, for they must feel that they don't belong here with us."

"I know it; they do look so different,"

Frances Harding, whose father was Chester's mayor, added. "It must be mortifying to dress just like everybody else," she continued.

The orphans did make a marked contrast to the others as they filed in the gate and through the school door. Dorothy's white felt hat could not keep her fair curls from blowing about her fairer face; and her pink sweater was so long as to almost reach the bottom of her skirts. Frances wore a crimson tam-o'shanter cap above her long, dark braids, and her red corduroy suit and tan boots made her look like a wood nymph, a bright creature dressed in the colors of scarlet leaves, and brown bark.

The two girls must have looked very winsome and attractive to the orphans. One little girl in blue at the end of the line stepped away from the others and went timidly up to Dorothy and Frances. She put out one hand and touched the soft pink wool of Dorothy's sweater shyly, as if even the touch of it were a delight. Dorothy drew away a little, but a faint flush of shame tinged her cheek, as the girl shrank back, almost as if she had been struck, and took her place in line.

"That's Molly Baxter," Dorothy said. "She's going to be at the head of our class before the year is out. Father says the Baxter

family, 'way back, came over in the Mayflower,
but there's nobody left now except Molly,
and there's no money either, so she had to
go on the town. I don't suppose she ever
had anything to wear so pretty as this sweater
in all her life."

"It's too bad, isn't it?" Frances said with a
kinder note in her voice. "She looks like a
little Puritan girl, doesn't she, in that long
blue dress and white hood?"

"O, that makes me think of next week—
Thanksgiving Day, Frances, and we're going to
have *such* a dinner!" Dorothy exclaimed, laughing gaily, as the two girl friends locked arms
and went into the schoolroom.

The whole atmosphere of the school was
charged with the spirit of the coming holiday.
The scholars had brought great branches of
oak and maple covered with bright leaves to
twine the school pictures of "The First Thanksgiving" and the "Pilgrims Going to Church."
Sprays of orange bittersweet filled a brass jar
on the teacher's desk, and a bunch of grain
had been put outside of one of the windows
to attract the birds.

It was history day. Dorothy's father, Professor Turner, stood on the platform and,
after the opening exercises, took charge of the
class.

"I want some one to recite the story of the Pilgrims' first Thanksgiving better than it has ever been recited before in the Blake School," he said. "Who will try?"

No one volunteered for a moment, not even Dorothy. Then a timid hand went up in the back of the room.

"Good!" Professor Turner said. "Molly Baxter ought to recite very well, for she comes of a Pilgrim family."

It seemed to little orphan Molly that twice the number of eyes pierced her that really did, as she stood up. She had loved the history lesson that told of the great, first family gathering for thanksgiving so long ago in New England. It had thrilled lonely Molly to the very heart, for it seemed so full of the plenty and love that had been denied her. As she began to recite, Molly's voice faltered. Then she forgot everything but her interest in the story. The class sat as still as mice, as they listened to the rise and fall of the little orphan girl's sweet voice.

"The days of spring and summer flew by," she said, "and autumn came to the Pilgrims. Never, in Holland or England, had they seen the like of the treasures that nature had given them. Their little farm plots had been blessed by sunshine and shower, so the Pilgrims, rejoicing, reaped their fruits, and housed them for the winter. They were filled with the spirit of thanksgiving, and so they decided to hold the first Harvest Home in New England.

"For a week they rested from work and feasted, and for three days they entertained the Indians. And the Indians brought them corn and venison, so all made merry together.

"It was a royal feast that the Pilgrims spread that first golden autumn, a feast worthy of their Indian guests. Kettles, skillets, and spits were overworked, and the knives and spoons made merry music on the pewter plates. The good governor put the vegetables that graced the table into rhyme. He said:

> " 'All sorts of grain which our own land doth yield,
> Was hither brought, and sown in every field;
> As wheat and rye, barley, oats, beans, and peas
> Here all thrive, and we profit from them raise.
> All sorts of roots and herbs in gardens grow,
> Parsnips, carrots, turnips, or what you'll sow,
> Onions, melons, cucumbers, radishes,
> Potatoes, beets, rhubarb and fair cabbages.'

"All the Pilgrims' jealousies and discontent were forgotten that first Thanksgiving Day. It made them better and braver to rest awhile and give thanks together. And it was a promise of other Thanksgivings to come."

Professor Turner did not try to hush the

subdued exclamations of pleasure from the class that followed Molly's last words. Neither did he try to stop the round of applause that came as she sat down. No one but Molly could have told the Thanksgiving story with so much feeling and charm. Even the orphans realized that as they sat up straighter with their pride that Molly belonged to them. All during the rest of the session the class found it difficult to settle down to problems in greatest common division and dry measure. In imagination they were Puritan children of long ago, measuring the good fruits and grains of the first harvest, and spreading the Thanksgiving table to share them with the Indians, that first Harvest Home.

Frances was waiting for Dorothy outside the school door at the end of the session.

"I've had a perfectly splendid idea for Thanksgiving, Dorothy," she said. Then she whispered something in her friend's ear. Dorothy listened intently, and then her face dimpled into a smile of delight.

"O, I think that would be lovely!" she said. "We'll do it. Tell the girls to meet at my house to-morrow afternoon to talk it over and ask them to wear their Camp Fire dresses. That will make it seem all the more real."

The two girls went out of the gate and up

the road together. They had to pass the
line of orphans, going home two by two, and
Dorothy called, "Molly, O, good-by, Molly!"

The little girl in blue turned, hardly be-
lieving that the pleasant words were meant
for her. When she saw that they really were,
for both Dorothy and Frances were waving
their hands to her, a smile of joy lighted her
face.

"Good-by. Thank you"—she half breathed
the last.

"Why, she's really pretty, isn't she?"
Dorothy said. "I never noticed how blue her
eyes are."

"And her hair wants to curl," Frances said,
"only they make her braid it all the time."

Thanksgiving was a real picture day.
Enough bright leaves were left to give it color,
and the sky was blue, without a cloud. The
golden sunshine made even the stubble in
the fields gleam, and the air was pungent
with the odors of fruit, and vegetables, and
bonfires.

It was like every other day at the Orphans'
Home though. There was the same routine
of getting up and dressing and going down to
breakfast by rule and time from the big dormi-
tories. The orphans would not go to school,
but certain tasks were detailed to them that

would fill the morning. There would be spare-ribs and apple sauce for dinner, with an orange for each child for dessert; but the table would still be bare of linen and set with the same thick white crockery and tin mugs. And it would not be a family feast for these little "all-alone" children.

Molly was all alive with the spirit of the day, though. Her eyes shone, and she burst into bits of song as she washed the faces and hands of the little ones and combed their hair before breakfast.

"It's my day!" she kept saying over and over to herself. "I'm one of the Thanksgiving children."

The thought sweetened Molly's breakfast porridge and made her fingers fly as she pared apples in the kitchen afterward.

"I'm pretending that it's the first Harvest Home," she said to herself, "and I'm getting ready for the dinner. There is ever so much to do because all those Indians are coming to share it with us. Why—" Molly looked out of the window at the sunny road, and then rubbed her eyes to see if she were dreaming. No, it was quite true; she could believe her eyes. Down the road toward the Orphan's Home marched a long line of Indians, brave in moccasins, fringed dresses, blankets and beaded headbands. They were everyday Indians, though, and carried, each one, a bag or basket. Dorothy and Frances led the line. They were the girls of the Blake School dressed in their Camp Fire costumes, and come to turn the Thanksgiving tables at the Orphans' Home. It was the Indians who would spread the feast for these small pilgrims who were as much alone and in need of friendship as those who came over in the Mayflower.

Molly ran out to meet them, and Dorothy came up to her with outstretched arms.

"It's all arranged with the matron," she explained. "We girls have brought over a Thanksgiving dinner, and we're going to set the table, and stay and eat it with you, and then play games in the afternoon. You are to help us, Molly, and it's going to be such fun!"

It was the best fun that the orphans had ever had. In almost no time the tables in the dining room were covered with snow-white cloths, along the edge of which the Camp Fire girls fastened trailing vines covered with crimson and yellow leaves. The wooden bowls from the kitchen were filled with rosy apples, purple grapes, russet pears, and nuts. The roasted turkeys and chickens that the girls had brought needed only to be warmed in

the oven to send out their delicious aroma.
There were little individual pumpkin pies and
mince pies and frosted cakes for all the orphans,
and even a package of homemade fudge for
each, tied with an orange ribbon and a spray
of bittersweet.

The Camp Fire girls, with Molly's help,
waited on table and then slipped into their
places between the orphans. It was surprising
how easy it was to get acquainted with each
other over the feast, and the tables looked
just like the pictures of the first Thanksgiving
dinner, the Indians in their bright costumes
sharing it with their more sober-clad neighbors.

The rule of no talking at meals that was
established at the home was lifted for this
happy day, and the dining room became suddenly alive with merry voices. When the
feast was over, Dorothy led them all into the
big living room, where an open fire was burn-
ing, and played the piano for singing, Molly
leading them, for she could sing as well as
recite history. The walls rang with "America,"
Martin Luther's hymn, "We Plough the Fields
and Scatter the Good Seed in the Land,"
"Over the River and Through the Woods,"
and "Columbia." Then they played Blind
Man's Buff, Going to Jerusalem, Puss in the
Corner, and the Farmer in the Dell, until

the short afternoon began to settle into golden dusk, and the setting sun told the Camp Fire girls that it was time for them to go home.

"We've had a beautiful time," Frances said. "So have we!" shouted a chorus of orphans.

"And we think we will come over every Saturday afternoon and see you," Dorothy said.

It was such good news that the Camp Fire girls could hardly say good-by because of the applause.

"Wasn't it a nice Thanksgiving?" Frances said as the girls went home, like a real band of Indians, between the field and trees.

"The best ever," Dorothy said, emphatically. "And aren't orphans nice?" she finished, happily.

CAPTAIN CHRISTY'S THANKSGIVING

"YOU'RE going beyond the life line, and the water's so rough you'll never be able to swim. O, Donald, don't! Come back. Don't go out so far!" the voice of the boy's little sister, Nan, shrilled out over the singing surf and was lost before it reached him.

The water of the bathing beach at Fishers Point was temptingly warm for so late in the season. Inside the boundaries of the safety line that the coast guard had stretched to mark the danger line there was a crowd of merry bathers. No one heard Nan's warning to her brother. No one saw his brown head bobbing on the far side of the rope or noticed his arm waved above the surf in a gay challenge and good-by. Donald was always daring in sport, but fighting ocean breakers was hard for a twelve-year-old boy who could count his strokes in still water. For a moment his white face showed above the waves. Then Donald disappeared from sight.

"Donald! O, save my brother, Donald!" Nan cried, plowing her way through the foam and up the beach.

"Boy gone down! Where is the coast guard?

He's gone down twice." The crowd knew now, and shouted, and made futile efforts to get out to him.

But a slim, gray boat suddenly swung out to sea from the upper end of the beach, nosing its way among the white caps like a setter scenting a fresh trail. It was manned and rowed by a crew of four sailors who sent it flying to the rescue. In its prow knelt an old man, his white hair and greenish gray coat making him look like Neptune. Suddenly he turned to give a quick order to the crew, and the boat came to a stop.

"Captain Christy! He'll get the boy all right." The words of the huddled bathers watching comforted Nan as she ran up the beach toward the pier from which the boat had started.

"He's been captain of the volunteer life guard for fifty years and can't remember how many lives he's saved. He's taught the boys and girls who come here in the summer to swim and pulled them out when they went in too deep."

Nan could hear no more, for she had reached the end of the tumble-down pier from which Captain Christy had started, and for which the boat was pulling now.

"Don't cry, little petrel!" the Captain cried

as he saw Nan in her black and white bathing suit, and stretching out her arms toward him. "The lad's here, a bit cold but not much the worse for his visit to the fishes."

As he spoke the boat slid alongside the pier and the Captain stepped out with Donald in his arms.

"Come up to my house," he said to Nan. "There's a fire going there and that's what the lad needs most now, heat and a hot drink." He strode ahead and Nan followed to the little weather-beaten shack that had been his only home for over half a century. It looked like the hulk of some old wreck washed up there on the beach, but it was bright with orange nasturtiums that bloomed in the tiny garden and a few flaming red chrysanthemums had opened like the sun setting in red over the sea.

Inside the shack there were a few comforts. The Captain laid Donald on the narrow bunk and poked the fire that smoldered in the little sheet-iron stove. Then he set a pot of some thick, savory stuff on it and stirred it as the savory smell began to fill the one tiny room.

Donald lay quietly for a moment. Then he opened his eyes and color came to his cheeks. All at once he pulled himself up to a sitting position.

"Clam chowder!" he said, looking about him.

"Yes, and you don't deserve it, you rash young scamp," Captain Christy said as he dipped up a brimming tin mug of the chowder and put it into Donald's eager hands. "What made you frighten your little sister so, and send me off on a chase through the surf after you when I was just putting a mess of chowder on to warm for my dinner?" But the Captain's harsh words ended in a chuckle as he gave Donald a resounding slap on his back. "I know what you were up to. You were trying to brave the sea, and that's a fine spirit to have if only you're sure enough of yourself. I must take you in hand and see that you learn how to swim better."

"O, thank you, Captain. I'm so much obliged," Donald said, getting on his feet.

"And so will mother and father thank you," Nan said. "We're going home in a week, but we'll come over and see you every day. We ought to go now, for some one may have told mother about Donald, and she would be so frightened."

Captain Christy went to the low door of the shack and looked out over the bare length of the beach and the cottages that would soon be empty.

"Going home!" he repeated. "You'll see lights in the streets at night, and you'll hear clanging bells on cars instead of the light-house lamp and the ringing of the bell buoy out in the cold."

"Don't you ever go away from here, not all winter?" Nan asked, wistfully.

"I haven't seen a city or kept a holiday in twenty years," Captain Christy said. "The summer folks go, but I stay here and keep warm with drift wood and listen for the cries from the wrecks. I'm as busy in the winter as in the summer, and terribly lonely, little mates."

The last days at the beach flew. Donald and Nan told Captain Christy good-by, boarded the little steamer that crossed to the mainland, took the train, and the family was at home once more in the city. The beginning of school made them forget the Captain waving good-by to them from the pier. It was near-ing Thanksgiving when their father read a newspaper headline aloud at the breakfast table.

"Fishing Boat Wrecked. Saved by Veteran Captain Christy of the Fishers Point Volunteer Guard." Then he laid down the paper. "That man's a hero," he exclaimed. "It's cold as Greenland up at the Point now, and he's close on seventy years old."

"He told us about the winter," Nan said.

"The lighthouse lamp is all he can see and the
bell buoy all he can hear." She thought a
minute. Then she ran over to her father's
chair. "I've had a splendid idea!" she said.
Then she suggested something to him.
"Donald and I were planning it for some time,
but wouldn't it be beautiful for Thanksgiving?
It could be done, couldn't it, daddy?"

Her father considered a moment. Then,
"Why, yes, it could. We will," he said.

Thanksgiving came in with a northeaster
at Fishers Point. The crew of the life boats
straggled down to the pier and stamped to
keep warm as they looked out over the choppy
sea.

"The steamer won't make the trip to-day,"
they said. "She hasn't come across in a week
now. Over yonder they're eating turkey in
the families. Wonder if they ever think of
the sailors who haven't seen the mainland
since cranberries were planted." Then they
fought the wind back to the Captain's and sat
around the stove, trying to make their own
cheer.

Captain Christy put in a few more hunks
of wood. As he bent over the wood basket
one of the men nudged another.

"See him hold his back," he whispered. "The
Captain's getting old."

"More lives than he can count, he's brought in," the other whispered back. They started to help the Captain, but they were interrupted by three shrill blasts of a whistle that sounded from the direction of the sea. New vigor in his old limbs, the Captain sprang to the door, opening it to a blast of wind that cut like a knife.

"It's the boat from the mainland," he shouted. "Maybe she's brought the mail. She's weathered the storm for Thanksgiving, boys!"

Then he got down his glasses. "She's unloading passengers! Who ever heard of that in a gale like this? They've got cargo with them!" At last he voiced the climax. "Shiver my timbers, lads, but the passengers and the cargo are coming this way!"

Donald came first, breathless from his run up the beach, his arms full, and followed by Nan.

"A happy Thanksgiving, Captain," he shouted. "We've come to spend it with you. Father had to pretty nearly buy the steamer to get us over, but here we are."

"And we've brought you a few things to make the winter easier," Nan said.

"And our chauffeur and father are bringing more things," Donald added.

Tinned meats and vegetables and coffee and milk and tea, blankets, books and magazines, a roasted turkey, a big cake, jellies—it did not seem possible that their arms could have brought so much comfort and good cheer.

Captain Christy could not speak at first. Then he brushed a suspicious mist from his eyes and reached out his hand to Donald.

"I'm more than grateful," he said huskily. "I know it's all the little mates' doing." Then he turned to his crew.

"Clear the decks, you lazy lubbers!" he laughed. "The ship's going to set sail for Thanksgiving."

They all managed to crowd around the little deal table that had a piece of sail cloth spread over it for a tablecloth and a bunch of coral in the center to decorate it. A tin pot of coffee on the stove and the warming turkey perfumed the shack.

"Isn't it jolly!" Donald whispered to Nan as he sat on an upturned keg in front of his tin plate.

"*Ssh!*" Nan said. "The Captain's going to ask a blessing."

"For strong boats and willing arms and for folks who remember us on the mainland, we give Thee thanks, our Lord of the sea," the Captain said.

There was a moment's hush and then Donald stood up.

"Father says I may give you this," he said, pulling from his pocket a leather box. He snapped it open and a flashing gold medal was disclosed on a satin cushion. "It's for you for being so brave, and he's arranged for you to come down to us whenever you feel like it, for we've got a room for you in the Sailors' Snug Harbor. It's a beautiful place, just for sailors, with ships going by all the time, and green lawns, and everybody will want to see you and hear you tell stories."

He stopped for breath.

"Three cheers for the Captain!" said one of his crew. They all shouted them, and Captain Christy pinned on his medal with shaking fingers.

"Thank you; thank you!" he said, tremulously, when they had quieted and begun on the turkey. "That Snug Harbor sounds fine. I'll come to it some day, but this Thanksgiving has put me in trim for a lot of storms yet, thanks to the little mates. That's how it puts heart in an old sailor when the mainland remembers him," he finished, gratefully.

THE COUNTRY MOUSE'S
THANKSGIVING

"OF course I am glad that Eleanor has come to live with us," Letty looked up from her pan of foaming dish suds to the curly yellow head bent low over a book in the sunshine of the back porch, "but somehow, Aunt Abby, she doesn't seem to fit in with me."

The patient invalid in the wheeled chair by the kitchen window smiled as she looked at Letty's wrinkled forehead and flushed cheeks.

"No, I guess Eleanor doesn't fit, yet," she said, "but maybe you wouldn't have fitted in your cousin's big house in the city, little Country Mouse, any better than she does here. We've got to realize that Eleanor hasn't had a mother since she can remember, and her father, until he lost his money, gave her everything that a girl could dream of wanting. I suppose, now Eleanor's lost her father, and everything, it will take her a little while to get used to our plain, country ways. But we'll try and keep her as happy as we can," Aunt Abby said, looking out too at the drooping little figure on the porch.

Letty wiped her brown hands and ran across the kitchen, throwing her arms around Aunt Abby's neck.

"You make me ashamed, Aunt Abby. I ought to like Eleanor better and try to help her, just for your sake. You've taken her in just as you took me when I was left without a home or anyone to look after me. I'll try, O, I will try to grow fond of Eleanor."

But as Letty finished speaking, Eleanor tossed down her book and came slowly into the kitchen. Was it imagination on Letty's part, or did her cousin look a little disdainfully at her hastily knotted-up hair and gingham morning apron.

"It's time to get ready for school, isn't it, Letty?" Eleanor said. "I think I'll go upstairs and change my dress. You won't mind if I don't wait for you, will you, Letty? I can't walk as fast as you do over these rough country roads."

Not a word had there been from Eleanor about helping with the breakfast dishes. Letty went back to the dishpan and dipped her hurrying hands in the suds again. She had to walk fast to school, usually, because she had so much to do at home before she started. She had not finished wiping the silver when Eleanor came downstairs ready. Her bright hair that always seemed to arrange itself, it was so curly, was daintily tied with a big pink bow. A long pink sweater covered Eleanor's white woolen middy suit, and she looked at her wrist watch as she started out.

"You'd better hurry, Letty, or you'll be late. I'll see you later. Good-by, Aunt Abby." Eleanor was off down the road, like a pink flower, blown by the November wind between the bare pastures on either side.

Letty sighed as she took off her apron and put on her last year's gray coat over her last year's dark blue serge dress. She knew that Eleanor had brought a supply of pretty clothes with her from the city when she had come to live with Aunt Abby, but even in the fudge apron that she had worn at a candy pull the week before Eleanor had looked the little city maid that she was. As she pulled her cap over her brown braids, Letty caught a glimpse of herself in the mirror that hung in the back entry. A round, kind, tanned little face looked back at her, but Eleanor's cheeks were like wild-rose petals. She saw two deep hazel eyes, like pools in the woods when the golden brown leaves are reflected in them, but Eleanor's eyes were as blue as the summer sky.

"It's true what Aunt Abby calls me. I am

only a Country Mouse, and I'll never be anything else," Letty said to herself as she tramped
down the road a good distance away from
Eleanor. "Maybe Eleanor's ashamed of me.
Perhaps that's the reason she doesn't play
with me often at recess, but goes with the girls
who drive over from Cedarville and wear the
kind of clothes that she does."

Tears filled Letty's eyes and made it hard
for her to see the road. Like a worm eating
its way into the heart of good fruit, the gnawing
hurt of jealousy had entered the spirit of the
little country cousin and was making her very
unhappy.

"I mustn't let Aunt Abby know, though,
how I feel," Letty thought as she reached
school and took her seat. "Any way I won't
have time to think of very much else but the
Thanksgiving dinner after to-day. Grandfather
and grandmother are coming, and they don't
know how well I can cook, or that I am going
to get every bit of the dinner myself. It's
going to be my nicest Thanksgiving Day because I'm going to show them that a girl twelve
years old can cook a Thanksgiving dinner,
from the oyster soup to the pumpkin pie.
Aunt Abby has given me her very precious
recipe for pumpkin filling that she got from
great-grandmother. Nobody anywhere around

will have so good a pumpkin pie as mine. Eleanor can recite poetry, and play the piano, but she can't *cook*." Letty gave her English Poets a rather vindictive push, sending the book into the back of her desk, and opened her history at the account of the sailing of the Mayflower.

The following days were so full of happy preparations for Thanksgiving on Letty's part that she almost forgot her hurt at Eleanor's seeming coolness toward her. Eleanor, from her first day, had been a great favorite in school. Not as clever as Letty, but full of a sweet winsomeness that attracted and made friends, she had so many invitations for fudge and nutting and sewing parties that she was not at home very much. When she was home she had to study, for she found the course in the district school more difficult than the one in the city. The long November evenings Eleanor spent curled on the floor at Aunt Abby's feet, her head in the invalid's lap and her hand clasped in the larger, thin one.

"Tell me more about father," Eleanor would beg, plainly homesick and finding little comfort in sensible little Letty, knitting in the lamplight.

"Even Aunt Abby likes Eleanor better than she does me," Letty thought, jealously. But the following day would find her too busy to have time for this thought.

Letty was always happiest in the kitchen. Now, as Thanksgiving approached, she was like a little brown thrush, bursting into song, as she worked. The quaint little house was as neat as a pin from attic to cellar. Andirons and candlesticks were polished, the dining room mantelpiece was aflame with jars of bittersweet vine and branches of black alder. The best gold and white china was taken down and the old silver was polished. The pantry shelves fairly groaned with golden pumpkin, ruby-red cranberries, nuts of every kind, Letty's own, spicy mincemeat, her sparkling jellies and the toothsome pickles that she had made in the summer. Hung in the cellar was the turkey, fat, white, and firm, and all ready for the stuffing that Letty felt no one could make as well as she.

Eleanor took a new interest in Letty's preparations. She had never known a real Thanksgiving in the country, and the frost on the corn fields, and the first flurry of snow seemed to put new spirit into the slender little figure.

The morning of the day before Thanksgiving Eleanor surprised Letty by coming into the kitchen with an apron on.

"I'm going to get the Thanksgiving dinner, Letty," she announced. "Father believed that every girl ought to know how to cook, so I went to cooking school for two winters. I'm going to surprise Aunt Abby; you can keep her out of the kitchen for me, can't you, Letty, while I am at work? She doesn't know how well I can cook and I want to surprise her. Dear Aunt Abby, I do so want to do something for her in return for all that she has done for me." Eleanor was prettier than ever, as she spoke, flushed with the pleasure of this new found, good motive.

"You shan't do it; it's going to be *my* Thanksgiving dinner"—the words rose to Letty's lips with a flare of temper, but she did not give them voice. She watched Eleanor's capable movements as she began her preparations. She rolled up her sleeves, got out just the necessary bowls and spoons, peeped into the flour and sugar barrels, and took a measuring cup in her hand.

"The pie crust first," she said to herself, "and then the cranberry jelly; and I'll make nut cakes if I have time. O, Letty, do go and read to Aunt Abby or something. You've got to keep her out of the kitchen all of to-day, and to-morrow, of course, while I'm roasting the turkey."

Perhaps Aunt Abby suspected the storm that was brewing in the house, and felt that it would be best for the little girls to settle it their own way. She was wise, and stayed in her own room, and Letty, heartbroken, wandered about the house with nothing to do but try and swallow the lump that would come in her throat. She could tell from the sounds and delicious odors which came from the kitchen that all was going well with the new little cook from the city. Eleanor was making jelly with the cranberries that she had washed, and filling piecrust with her mince meat. The nuts she was putting in her cake, Letty had cracked. The tears would come to Letty's eyes, but she brushed them away as Eleanor's radiant face appeared in the doorway.

"O, Letty," she exclaimed in a whisper, "I'm getting along finely, only I don't quite understand the dampers in this coal stove. You see I've been used to cooking on a gas range. Do come out and show me about them."

"I'm not going to. I want you to spoil things so Aunt Abby and grandfather and grandmother will find out that you can't cook as I can"—again the words flashed into Letty's mind, but she did not speak them. For a moment she hesitated, frowning. Then, unable to resist the lure of Eleanor's happy face, she answered her: "All right. I'll come out and show you. It's easy enough to manage the oven once you know how."

But Eleanor had let the fire burn low, and Letty had to put on more coal and watch it until it came up again. Then Eleanor turned to her. "I've got crust enough for two more pies, Letty, and nothing to put in them. Do you know how to make a good pumpkin filling? We never learned how to make pumpkin pie in school, but I could make it easily if only I had a recipe." She waited eagerly, her dainty, floury hands outstretched.

Letty's mind suddenly gave place to a strong desire for revenge. Thanksgiving dinner would not be complete without thick, golden slabs of great-grandmother's pumpkin pie. She could tell Eleanor that she could make it, but had no recipe. But, almost as soon as the jealous plan came to Letty, it was displaced in her mind by a strange, new feeling of helpfulness toward the little stranger cousin. Eleanor's blue eyes were so pleading. Her new joy in doing something for others was genuine.

"Yes, I have a splendid rule for pumpkin pie. It's a very old family recipe," was what Letty said as she pulled a piece of folded, yellow paper from her pocket and handed it to Eleanor. "I'm glad to let you use it."

"Cream, eggs, sugar—my! but it sounds good," Eleanor said as she unfolded the paper and hastily read the recipe. "Now, run along to Aunt Abby, Letty. The fire's going nicely, and I like to be alone when I cook."

It was a white-and-crimson Thanksgiving Day, white with the first deep snow and bright with the red glow of the fire. The table was daintily set by Eleanor's own hand. It had been her thought, too, to lay a great wreath of trailing pine and bittersweet in the center of the white cloth with a basket of rosy apples and oranges inside it. Never had they seen such a pretty center piece.

Aunt Abby in her wheeled chair and grandfather and grandmother made a circle of happiness around the table. The two girls, Letty in one of Eleanor's blue smocks and with a big blue bow on her hair, waited on the beloved guests. The dinner was perfect, from the crisply browned turkey to the pumpkin pie that almost melted in its rich, yellow toothsomeness.

Grandfather drew a sigh of satisfaction as he finished the last flake of the crust.

"Who made this pie?" he asked.

There was a second's silence and then Letty spoke, bravely.

"Eleanor made it, grandfather. She cooked the whole dinner herself."

Wonderful was the effect of the brave confession upon the little girl who had made it. It seemed to transform her whole feeling for her little stranger cousin. She was no longer jealous of her, but rejoiced with her in all that she had been able to do to help with the Thanksgiving cheer. And her mood was contagious. Eleanor ran over to Letty, throwing her arms around her.

"Not all alone, grandfather. I never could have cooked the Thanksgiving dinner if Letty hadn't helped me. And it's her pumpkin pie, really. I only followed the recipe that she gave me."

"Well, well." Grandfather smiled over his spectacles at the two little girls, arm in arm, and closer even than that in their new-found companionship. "That's the way it ought to be," he said. "It's just as important to do team work making a pie as anything else. And, seeing that you two girls are getting along so well together, how about starting college together one of these days? I think it can be managed," he finished, with an even wider smile.

"O, Letty, I feel as if I were just beginning to get acquainted with you," Eleanor said as the two girls snuggled together in front of the open fire Thanksgiving night. "Do you know, I've always been a little afraid of you, because I felt as if you knew so much more than I do, but that's all gone now."

"It's gone from me too," Letty said, happily, as she smoothed Eleanor's shining hair and looked, without a pang of jealousy, into her sweet, upturned face. What was gone, Letty did not say, but Thanksgiving had taken away from her all thought of envy and hard feeling.

THE CHRISTMAS TREE CLUB

"WE'RE a cheerful enough Club," Molly Newton said, laughingly, as she bit into a thick square of freshly made fudge, "but I don't think that anyone in school thinks of us as toilers exactly."

The other girls, gathered in the Newtons' cheery living room in front of an open fire, looked up, a bit surprised, as Molly set the plate of candy on a table and went on. "We named ourselves the Cheerful Toilers' Club, thinking that we'd do something for our class or for somebody or something that needed us here in town; and you all know, girls, that the only toiling we've done has been to give ourselves a good time."

"We made perfectly splendid fudge this afternoon; three kinds too—plain, marshmallow, and nut," Betty Fraser said, thoughtfully, shaking out her yellow curls as she spoke.

"And we've eaten it nearly all up," Molly replied, accusingly.

"We cross stitched some beautiful work bags last week, some with wreaths, and some with flower baskets, and some with initials," Mildred Hardy said.

"Yes, and we planned them for the church fair Christmas week; and when we finished them they were so pretty that we decided to keep them ourselves," Molly added.

"Well, how about the Halloween party that we gave in our barn?" Judith Dexter asked, her dark eyes flashing. "We invited a whole lot of girls who don't belong to the Club, and we had charades and games, and cakes and chocolate that we made ourselves?"

"I know, Judith. We all worked just as hard as we could, but I don't believe it was the right kind of Club toiling," Molly answered, soberly. "We had a good time ourselves, in just the way we wanted to; and we asked only the girls that are in our set. I heard Jean speaking about us at recess yesterday. She said that she wished she could belong to the Cheerful Toilers' Club. She thought she ought to, because she'd been working at home, and trying to be cheerful about it, ever since she could remember.

"But she understood, she said, that the Club wasn't for the girls in the mill end of town. It was just for us."

"Well, Jean was right. It isn't. It is just for us," Betty broke in, but Molly threw her arm about the little girl's shoulder and drew her close to her as she laid soft fingers on Betty's pouting red lips.

"What I wanted to ask you this afternoon, girls, is if we can't change the Club, name and everything, until after Christmas anyway. I've got a perfectly splendid plan in my head and I want to have a chance to see how it works. Jean gave me an idea"—Molly stopped a minute as the girls frowned and shook their heads at the mention of the little French girl.

None of them had been able to quite understand the colony of foreign children that the newly built factory had brought to the town. There was Jean with her gay colors, dark, eager face, and a clever mind that sent her to the head of her class at once. Hilda, too of German parentage, had been left to study and play by herself during her six months with them. They could see her now, her pink cheeks flushing a deeper tint, and pulling her long flaxen braids in embarrassment when the town girls refused to speak to her in the school yard. They had not meant to be unkind to the strangers, but they did not understand their ways, their clothes, or their broken speech.

"Well, if we've got to take in the girls like Jean we might as well give up the Club at once," Judith said decisively.

"O, wait a minute, girls, please! You don't

understand; do let me try to explain," Molly begged, sitting down in the midst of the group around the fire and looking toward the door to see if anyone were listening. Then she unfolded her Christmas plan for the new Club.

The fire crackled, and the winter wind blowing down the chimney brought drifting echoes of silvery-toned sleigh bells. Through the window the girls could see the gathering snowstorm with its white, starry snow flakes. It all added charm to Molly's plan, which seemed, as she explained it a little at a time, to be quite the best fun that the Club had thought of yet. When she finished there was a shout, and a wreath of many arms about their kind little president's neck.

"We'll do it!"

"It's going to be so jolly!"

"Won't it be a surprise!"

"We'll begin to-morrow!"

That was how the new Club began.

It was fortunate that the Christmas holidays included several days before Christmas. There was so much for the girls to do. Molly's father owned the town lumber yard, and she persuaded him to lend her a sleigh and a wood cutter for one afternoon. She and the rest of the Club piled into it and had a merry ride to the woods that lay at the edge of the town. When they

came back their arms and the sleigh were full
of trailing lengths of ground pine, sprays of
hemlock, and branches of laurel. They brought
a tall, beautifully shaped fir tree that was
hidden in the lumber yard until the Club
should need it. The greens the girls twined
into long ropes and wound into wreaths with
deft fingers.

Mildred established herself as the Christmas
seamstress in the Club's secret sewing bee.
She scoured the attics of the town for cast-off
finery and pieces of colored cloth that could
be used for their needs. The girls consulted
old pictures, and even persuaded Miss Thomp-
son, the town seamstress, to cut patterns for
some of the garments that they couldn't
fashion themselves. It was surprising how
much they could do with a little. An old
white tarleton dress made all the candy bags
they needed, cut and stitched in the shape
of fat little stockings; and the town candy
man filled them, free, when they told him the
Club's secret.

Cotton-batting, dotted with black worsted
stitches, made ermine that looked like real fur.
Gilt paper stars glued to an old white blanket
made it into a royal cloak. Tinsel stars, strings
of popcorn and cranberries, and such useful
gifts as warm mittens and woolen mufflers

grew in the girls' fingers and those of their mothers and grandmothers who shared their secret.

Judith's house resounded with the Club girls' voices as they practiced Christmas carols; and above them, like a lark's clear note, could be heard Jean's sweet voice.

What could it mean? the girls who did not share the secret wondered. They watched the houses of the Club girls to see what new mystery might appear in each window or front door. No one thought of going near the schoolhouse, closed for the holidays. That was how the Club was able to make its secret preparations for Christmas Eve without any one seeing them.

It was a wonderful Christmas Eve. A heavy fall of snow, a cold snap without wind, and an early starlight made a shining, white world for the coming of the Holy Child into the hearts of men.

A flash of light in the big, white schoolyard and the glimpse of green that late Christmas shoppers had as they passed was the first hint of the surprise.

"There's a big Christmas tree, *outdoors*, in the school yard."

"It's lighted with red and yellow electric bulbs."

"It's for all the school children"—the news

was winged through the town as if a Christmas angel had carried it.

The schoolyard was open to anyone who wished to come. The children from the factory end of town came, shyly, but they found the teachers waiting for them and a welcome among the others.

It was a beautiful tree. Just to look at it was to feel a Merry Christmas in one's heart. As if it grew there, it stood in the center of the snowy yard, its myriad of lights shining and twinkling like so many stars. About it, marked by a rope of evergreen, was a great green circle and wreaths of greens were hung on the school fence. Every one was quite satisfied and content to only look at the outdoor Christmas tree, but suddenly a strange procession wound into the schoolyard.

Every one had been inclined to make fun of the little white donkey that Jean's family had brought to their tiny home, and that Jean sometimes drove into town. Now the donkey, with Jean, the Christmas Herald, riding him, seemed a lovely part of the Christmas pageant. Jean's dark eyes shone like stars. Her long brown hair, lying loosely on her shoulders, curled like a soft cloud beneath the gilt crown she wore. Her white cloak, spangled with stars, almost covered the little donkey.

She carried a silver trumpet that she blew to announce the coming of the girls who walked behind her.

Gretchen came next, quite transformed by her scarlet cloak and hood, and with a bag of gifts, for she was Father Christmas. Following her came other quaintly garbed girls; a group of Christmas waifs, Mrs. Santa Claus, the Russian Babouscka, Piccola of the quaint old story—each in a simple costume that was slipped over their warm wraps. In one respect all were alike, though: each girl carried in her hand a tiny Christmas bough.

When they reached the schoolyard, Jean dismounted and they all stood beside the green circle about the tree. It was Jean's sweet voice that led them in the old Christmas songs and carols that all knew, and so all could join in singing. "Hark, the Herald Angels Sing," "Carol, Brothers, Carol," "Once in Royal David's City"—the music echoed through the schoolyard in the light of the Christmas stars.

Then Gretchen emptied her bag of gifts and stripped the tree for the Christmas guests. There was a tiny gift for each child, if it were only a stocking of sweets or a rosy apple.

Last of all, Molly stood in front of the tree. Her Mrs. Santa Claus costume of white cap, scarlet frock, and white apron made every one listen as she raised her hand for silence, and then spoke to the others:

"I think you all know that a few of us girls had a Club," she said, "and we called it the Cheerful Toilers. Well, we found out a while before Christmas that we weren't doing the best kinds of things in the Club, and we needed more members, especially girls that we want to know better.

"So we changed the Club, and it's ever so much bigger, and better, and more exciting now. It's called the Christmas Tree Club, because a Christmas tree stays green and grows almost all over the world. Jean has helped us think a lot. O, you tell the rest, Jean," and Molly pulled the little French girl to her side.

The children had not known how winsome Jean was. She looked like her namesake, the girl soldier of France, as she spoke to them.

"In my country," Jean said, "we have our happiest times out of doors, and together. That is what the Club will do; it will help us all to keep our good holidays together and give happiness to others. We will sing around the flag, and we will play about a May pole. When there is no holiday we will try and make happy all those children who are sorrowful."

As the little girl stopped, a bit frightened at speaking to so many, her teacher finished:

"So this Christmas tree will be green in our hearts and lives until another year," she said.

"Hurrah for the Christmas Tree Club! Hurrah! Hurrah!" the shout pealed out through the schoolyard in a merry Christmas chorus.

"Wasn't it wonderful?" Molly asked as the girls of the old Club crowded about their little Christmas Herald on the way home.

"O, yes!" Jean sighed, happily. "And now there will be no more lonesomeness among us."

TRUSTY'S CHRISTMAS

A T first Emily and Newton were not quite
sure whether or not they liked living
opposite the hospital.

Their father had bought the land and built
their big, rambling white house on the other
side of the street from the hospital because
it was so quiet. But the brother and sister
saw the ambulance coming almost every day
to the hospital and a steady stream of doctors
and nurses going and coming. Glimpses inside,
when the curtains were drawn from the windows, showed row upon row of white beds.
There were children in the beds too, boys and
girls who seemed to be of the ages of Emily
and Newton—ten and twelve.

"I just can't bear to look over at the hospital, mother," Emily said one day.

"Change your spectacles, dear," her mother
advised. "You have been wearing blue goggles
ever since we moved into the new house here.
Put on a pair of rose-colored glasses and note
what a difference it will make with what you
see."

Emily laughed and then told Newton what
their mother had said. It did make things

seem very different, though, to look at them in a rosy light. The hospital beds emptied themselves almost as fast as they were filled. Happy, well boys and girls and grown-ups left the hospital with their friends almost every day and there were so many beautiful things happening there to watch.

The flowers that were carried into the hospital made one think of gardens that bloomed all the year. At Thanksgiving time bulging packages and baskets packed to overflowing were taken in. Before Christmas every window in the hospital was gay with a wreath of holly. Echoes of laughter and bright glimpses of greens in the convalescent ward drifted across the street. The brother and sister began to go and come from school on the hospital side of the street, for their dread of it had changed to interest.

That was how they came to get acquainted with the blind man who sold apples and oranges at the hospital gate.

"He's always smiling, even if he is blind," Emily told them at home. "He has his fruit in a tray that hangs from his shoulder by a strap and he can make change by just feeling of the money "

"You ought to see his little dog, Trusty, though," Newton exclaimed. "He's nothing but a street dog, a fox terrier, but he knows as much as a human being. He leads his master to the hospital gate in the morning, and takes him home again at night. He holds a tin pail in his teeth for the money and he never leaves his master a minute during the day to go off and play with other dogs."

The two children began to stop every day to buy fruit for their school luncheon from the blind man. They found out that his name was Billings, and, of course, they had learned the dog's name.

"He's all the family I've got," Mr. Billings explained. "I have had him for ten years now. When we get through the day's work we go home and have a fine supper together, Trusty sitting on one side of the kitchen table and I on the other. He's my eyes and my best friend, is that little dog. I don't know what I'd do without him."

It was not long before Christmas that Newton heard sounds of a dog fight as he neared home on his way from school. It made slight impression upon him until shrill yelps of pain were mingled with the barks, and above this came a man's voice calling, "Help! Help!"

Newton ran as fast as he could in the direction of the hospital. When he reached the gate his worst fears were realized.

Trusty was in the grip of a bull dog. The bull dog, his low-hung jaw watering, had attacked Trusty apparently out of spite because the smaller dog would not give up his post by the gate. Trusty, though wiry and active, was unable to stand against such a foe, and th⸍ fierce animal, as is customary, had gotten a hold and was keeping it. He had set his teeth in Trusty's leg.

Tears were running down Mr. Billings's wrinkled cheeks. "Save Trusty, save my poor little Trusty," he begged. "I can't see where he is or I could do it myself."

If Newton had stopped to consider danger, he would probably have failed, but with a stick he went at the bull like a whirlwind. The bull dog, in turn, through sheer surprise, loosened his hold and trotted off, pretty much as if he were not interested in chewing up small dogs after all.

Emily came up then, breathless, and eager to help.

"It's all right, Mr. Billings," she assured Trusty's trembling master.

It was not all right though. Moaning with the pain of a leg almost severed by laceration and fracture, the brave little dog lay in the street, a trail of blood showing on the freshly fallen snow.

"We must do something with him or he'll die," Emily said to her brother.

Newton thought a second. Then using his handkerchief as a tourniquet he stopped the bleeding to some extent, and picking up the little dog in his arms, started boldly in the hospital gate.

"I'm going to take him to father's friend, Dr. Whitman," Newton said. "Maybe he can take care of him in the laboratory where they have the monkeys and frogs. Anyway, I'll ask him."

Emily, stifling the sob that choked her as she saw Trusty lay his head on Newton's shoulder and shut his faithful brown eyes, went over to the blind man. She picked up the several apples and oranges which had fallen from his tray in the excitement and put a friendly little hand in his.

"My brother is taking your little dog into the hospital," she said. "Don't worry about him, and just stay here for the rest of the day. Newton and I will take you home to-night and we will start for school early enough in the morning to get you and bring you here. We'll do that every day and take you home until we know how Trusty is coming out."

Inside the hospital a group of half-amused

nurses and two or three young physicians surrounded Newton and his wounded burden.

"It can't be done. He'll have to be chloroformed," they agreed, but just then the surgeon, Dr. Whitman, appeared.

"Newton Maxwell!" he exclaimed. "And your father and I were in college together! So you've brought in a friend who needs us, Newton." He hesitated a second. Then he motioned to an orderly to take Trusty. "It is rather a precedent to establish," he said, "but I think it can be arranged."

And it was.

Mr. Billings had a two-room cottage down near the river. It was as neat as a pin, and Emily and Newton laughed merrily when they saw Trusty's high chair, his bowl and plate marked "For a Good Dog," and a bunk by the side of the stove where he slept. It was hard for all three of them to be cheerful during the next few days, but Mr. Billings's gratitude delighted the children, and their hopes for Trusty comforted him. Mr. Billings was at his post every day, and he had never done so much business before. Everyone who had seen the little dog taking care of his master stopped to inquire how he was, and no one went on without buying an orange or an apple.

Their first Christmas opposite the hospital

found Emily and Newton with only a half
interest in their own gifts.   They hurried
through breakfast and put on their coats and
caps immediately afterward ready to go down
and get Mr. Billings.   They ran all the way,
so eager were they, calling breathlessly to each
other as they went.

"Isn't it wonderful!"

"Won't he be surprised!"

But they found the blind man only half
interested in the "Merry Christmas!" they
shouted the moment they were inside his
door.   They emptied the Christmas box they
had brought him and put a warm muffler, a
pair of fur gloves, and a big package of fragrant
coffee into his hands; but even these gifts
failed to rouse him.

"I suppose we better start for the hospital
soon, Mr. Billings," Newton said at last.

The blind man shook his head, feeling his
way about the room and touching Trusty's
bed and chair.

"I can't go," he said at last.   "You've been
very kind to me, and I thank you from my
heart, but I can't tell you what these days
have been to me without my little dog.   I
listen for his barking and there isn't a sound;
and I can't bear to stand in the street alone,
not able to reach out my hand and know that

Trusty's there to lick it. We've been together ten years, Trusty and I."

Emily took Mr. Billings's hands in both of hers and entreated, although there was a catch in her voice.

"Please come, Mr. Billings. It's Christmas Day, and so many visitors will be going to the hospital and wanting to buy your fruit."

But the blind man still resisted.

"My little dog was there with me last Christmas," he said. "You don't tell me anything about him; maybe he's dead this Christmas."

"He isn't dead," Emily assured Mr. Billings.

"Please come," Newton begged. "We've got a secret about Trusty, Mr. Billings; that's why we haven't told you. Do come."

So, in the end, the children led the blind man to his place by the hospital gate.

They were exultant in their glad excitement. The children's ward had been told of the news on Christmas Eve, and it almost eclipsed the big Christmas tree, aglow with electric light bulbs and weighted down with gifts, that stood in the open space between the beds.

"You wait here, Mr. Billings," Emily and Newton said when they reached the hospital gate. "We will be out in a minute." Then they went inside the hospital to get Trusty.

Dr. Whitman himself brought Trusty to

them. The dog wore a red woolen sweater, the gift of the nurses, he had a new leather collar, and a large variety of Christmas bones contributed no little to his contentment. Dr. Whitman was evidently pleased with his achievement in dog surgery and Trusty's own satisfaction was plainly seen as he took his triumphant way through the children's ward, receiving a greeting from every bed.

Outside his blind master waited. The world had never seemed so dark to him; no sun, no vision of sparkling snow and Christmas greens, no dog friend at his side—but, what was that? Mr. Billings's trained ears detected a familiar patter of feet coming down the stone pavement from the hospital. He was puzzled, though, at an unfamiliar sound. *Trot, tap; trot, tap.* That was the rhythm the footsteps made, coming nearer and nearer.

"Trusty?" his master called.

He put out his hand and a wet, warm tongue brushed it; then a happy wriggling, barking dog was in Mr. Billings's arms. He felt of Trusty.

"It's all right. You won't hurt him if you touch it, and he can use it just as well as he can the other three," Newton said.

"He's the very first dog in the world, I guess, to have a wooden leg." Emily added. "They had to cut off the leg that the bull dog bit, but he's got a fine, strong wooden one in its place; Dr. Whitman made Trusty as good as new!" she finished, joyously.

Tap, tap, Trusty jumped out of his master's arms and began circling around him wagging his tail as hard as he could and showing how well he could walk with his wooden leg.

"Bow, wow! I'll take you home myself to-night, dear master," Trusty seemed to say as the children left the two alone together.

"It's the jolliest Christmas we ever had, isn't it, Newton?" Emily asked.

"I should say so!" her brother said, "and all on account of living across the street from a hospital."

MARJORY'S CHRISTMAS SHOP

"I KNOW having father in the army this year makes it a more wonderful Christmas than any before," Marjory sighed, "but it is hard on the little ones not to have the least hope of seeing Santa Claus," she finished, with a half sob in her voice.

Her mother looked up from the lamp-lit table where she was mending a pile of small stockings.

"The twins and baby can stand it just as bravely as a little girl I know, who has always enjoyed being Santa Claus herself more than receiving gifts," she said, her tired face showing white but very tender in the circle of light. "I am sorry, dear." She drew the little daughter close to her and dropped a kiss on her soft brown hair.

Marjory brushed away the tears that would spill over her brown eyes, and tried to smile. "It is that, Mumsy. The twins tried to call up the fireplace chimney to Santa Claus last night. Joey wants a fire engine, and Tom a train of cars. And the baby needs a lot of useful things for Christmas—leggings, and a sweater—and I did want to get them for her."

Mrs. Harding put her arms close around Marjory. "It is going to be a hard Christmas," she said, "and we shall not be able to hang up stockings or have a tree, but we must remember how many families there are like us all over the land this year. Father is giving the greatest gift of all, his service to his country, and you can do the same sort of giving of service, little daughter. You do, dear, every day," she added. "A great many families right here in town would be grateful for a pair of hands like yours, so busy and so clever."

Marjory was silent a moment, thinking, then she went over to the other side of the table and sat down, still thinking. Suddenly she lifted a radiant face to her mother, and spoke.

"I've got an idea about something I want to do for Christmas, Mumsy," she said. "You gave it to me just now, but I'd like to have it a secret, if you are willing, until I know how it turns out. May I have the front room, all for myself, until Christmas Eve, please? I don't want you to even peep in. I'll try not to let the secret interfere with anything I need to do to help you. May I try it?"

"Of course, Marjory," her mother said. "I can always trust you, dear, and I will try and make the housework as light as I can so as to give you more time."

The Hardings' house stood on the main street of the town where a good many people passed it each day. And almost everyone knew and loved the Hardings, and missed Dr. Harding when he felt it his duty to join the army. So it was with a great deal of interest that the neighbors and school children read the sign that Marjory painted and put in the window of the front room the fortnight before Christmas. It was lettered in scarlet and gold on a white card with a border of holly done in colors around the edge. It read:

MARJORY HARDING. HER SHOP
FOR CHRISTMAS SERVICE
OPEN UNTIL EIGHT O'CLOCK
IN THE EVENING
DO COME IN

If Mrs. Harding saw the sign first of all, she did not say so. She arranged for Marjory to be free of the dishwashing, and she took the twins and the baby out herself to see the Christmas toys so that Marjory might be free to carry out her secret plan. She shut her ears, too, to the pealing of the front door bell that showed how interested passers-by were to see the interior of the queer shop. From the morning when the shop was opened it was patronized.

It looked like Christmas. Marjory had put
a bowl of holly on the center table and sat behind it in her red serge skirt and white middy
blouse, with a bow of red on her hair.   But
the Christmas shop looked businesslike too.
There were a big workbasket, a blank book
for taking orders, a tin cash box, and signs
painted in red and green were hung on the
wall.   They helped to explain what Marjory's
shop was for.

The workbasket was full to overflowing, and
Marjory's needle was flying the morning that
old Mrs. Chapin came into the Christmas shop.
Her coachman had brought her to the door,
and she looked with a kind smile in her twinkling
eyes at the little shopkeeper.

"Well, Marjory, what are you up to now?"
she asked as she raised her lorgnette and in-
spected the pile of bright scraps on the table.

"O, I am having such a good time as well as
filling orders, Mrs. Chapin," Marjory said.
"This is my first order, dressing dolls for the
Blodgett children. Mrs. Blodgett can't make
dolls' clothes, and her two little girls are old
enough now so that they want dolls with
clothes that will come off. Just look, aren't
they dear?—yellow hair and blue eyes for
Dorothy, and brown hair and brown eyes for
Pauline! And each doll is going to have an

entire set of underwear with buttons and buttonholes, a gingham dress for everyday, and an embroidered white dress for best. I am making them sweaters and caps and coats—" Marjory stopped for breath. Then she finished: "And Mrs. Blodgett is going to pay me ten cents an hour for the sewing."

Mrs. Chapin lifted one of the dolls' garments, looking at the fine stitches. "I see," she said. "You are helping others by doing the Christmas work that they find difficult to do. I think it is an excellent plan, and I am going to use the Shop for Christmas Service right away if I may. There are so many children and grown folks that I want to give to at Christmas—the Sunday school children, and the old folks out at the Poor Farm, and the grocer's boy, and the butcher's boy, and I don't know how many others. I always believe that half the pleasure of a Christmas present comes in its wrappings. You know what I mean, Marjory, lots of crinkly tissue paper and red ribbon bows, and bunches of holly, and Christmas seals. I want my gifts to look just as Christmas-y as they possibly can, but I haven't time to wrap them all myself. If I bring them down here, with the wrappings, will you do them up for me, Marjory? I will pay you five cents each for them."

"O, Mrs. Chapin!" It was all Marjory could say, but her happy face told the rest as she opened the door for the old lady and watched her drive away. It seemed no time at all until the sleigh was back and the coachman made several trips into the Christmas Shop, his arms loaded with gifts and bright materials for wrapping them.

The dolls' clothes were finished, and Marjory pressed them neatly, dressed the dolls, and closed the Shop for fifteen minutes while she took them home. Then she began the fun of making Mrs. Chapin's Christmas gifts look prettier than they ever had before.

"Red tissue paper ought to be tied with this gold ribbon," she said to herself as she worked. "I will save the green and the red ribbon to tie the things I wrap in white. The games and picture books for the children in the infant department ought to have Santa Claus seals and gold stars and Christmas stocking tags on them. The books for the older boys and girls shall have big ribbon bows and bunches of this beautiful artificial holly. How pretty they do look!" she said as she looked over the pile of bright parcels packed in hampers and ready to be called for. She counted them, and set down some figures in her blank book.

"O," Marjory clasped her hands in happiness as she read the result. "Seventy-five packages wrapped for Mrs. Chapin at five cents a piece —three dollars and seventy-five cents! O, I do believe that we're going to have a Christmas after all," she said aloud.

"Well, it looks like Christmas," the minister said as he came in and overheard Marjory's joyful comment. "I just heard about my little parishioner's Shop for Christmas Service from Mrs. Chapin, and I have come to see if I may ask for some much-needed help. I hope you can give it to me?" he asked.

"I will try, sir," Marjory said, dimpling with pleasure.

The minister set a box of envelopes and cards down on the table. "These are the invitations for the Christmas Sunday School Tree," he explained, "and they all have to be addressed. Can you write a good plain hand, little lady of the Christmas Shop?" he asked.

"I took a prize for penmanship in school last term," Marjory answered, proudly.

"Good!" the minister exclaimed. "Then you are just the one I need. Here is the list of addresses in this book, and here are the stamps. I will trust you to do the entire work of sending out the invitations and we have a fund for clerical work of this kind out of which

I can pay you twenty-five cents a dozen for addressing and mailing the cards. There are as many as ten dozen invitations, including the fathers and mothers."

No sooner had Marjory finished the addressing than her Sunday school teacher came to the Shop with some candy boxes to be covered with bright cretonne for the class. When the boxes were finished, they seemed too pretty to be filled with store candy, so Marjory made fudge and nut squares to put in them. There was a little extra fudge and it sold at once. with orders for more. Busy and happy, the days flew by on the wings of snowflakes and to the tune of the singing of Marjory's joyous heart. Before she knew it Christmas Eve had come, and the Shop was closed.

The twins and the baby were in bed, and Marjory and her mother were playing Santa Claus in the living room. Breathing the odor of the woods, the Christmas tree that Marjory had bought with her earnings stood beside the fireplace. It was hung from the tip to the lowest branch with those glittering trimmings that a Christmas tree wears with so much grace.

"I bought ever so many gilt stars, mother," Marjory said, "for they make me think of the star of Bethlehem. And this silver tinsel

is like moonbeams, and the gold tinsel like
sunbeams shining down on the tree. Here are
some glass icicles and some frost powder: O,
don't they sparkle! These are candy fruits,
apples, and pears, and peaches. We'll put
Joey's fire engine down here on the floor under
the tree. Won't he be surprised! He didn't
expect a fireman's suit and a hook and ladder
too."

"No, indeed," her mother said, "and Tom
doesn't expect a train of cars that will really
go, and tracks, and a switch. They can't go
under the tree, dear. We'll have to set them
out in the middle of the room."

"All right, mother," Marjory said. "You
lay the tracks while I put something deep down
here in the tree that I don't want you to see,"
and she hid the soft lace collar the Shop had
earned for her mother's gift.

"Now the baby's things. Won't she look
just like a little snow elf in these leggings and
sweater?" Marjory went on. Then she turned
to the sign in the window. "I ought to take
it out," she said, "for I have closed the Shop,
but I do want to leave it up until Christmas
morning. I know what I will do." Marjory
lighted a candle and set it in the window sill
underneath the sign. "I will leave the curtain
up and this candle here to show everybody

who has been so kind to me what my Shop has done for the Harding family." She stopped a moment with a little catch in her voice, "For the Hardings who are here for Christmas," she finished.

The words were scarcely spoken when there was a sharp ring at the door bell. Marjory ran to open it. A blue-coated messenger stood in the snow outside.

"Twenty-eight Elm Street," he said. "A telegram for Mrs. Harding. I couldn't see the house number, it was so dark, until you put that light in the window." He pointed to the Christmas candle.

"Father is—" Marjory could not say any more as her mother opened the yellow envelope with trembling fingers.

"Father is coming home on leave. He will be here to-morrow morning," her mother said.

"And it was the sign of the Christmas Shop that helped bring us his message," Marjory said. "Was there ever such a wonderful Christmas, Mumsy, as ours will be?" she asked.

"Or such a wonderful Santa Claus as you, dear?" her mother finished, putting tender arms around the brave little lady of the Christmas Shop.

THE NEW YEAR'S TREASURE SHIP

"IT'S hard to think of any way to celebrate a holiday that comes so close to Christmas, isn't it?" Jack Newton said, as the group of boy and girl classmates stood on the snowy path that led from the church door to the street. "It was fine of Dr. Richards to say that our class could probably think of something better to do this New Year's than any year before, but what is it going to be?"

"Go calling," Doris Richards retorted, laughingly, "only that cuts us girls out, and what's the use of you boys coming to call when we see you every day in school?"

"We might make good resolutions," Jack suggested, "but Dr. Richards told our class last Sunday that he thought every day in the year ought to be a good resolution day, not just New Year's. How do you feel about this different celebration we've got to think up, Bruce?" he asked of a slender, tanned boy who was listening to the others, but had not spoken yet.

"I was remembering last New Year's Day over in Japan," Bruce Richards said. "Father had a mission, you know, just a little way

out of Tokio, and so Doris and I had a fine
chance to see the celebration. Flags were
flying everywhere in honor of the treasure
ship that is supposed to sail into the harbor
on New Year's Eve. It isn't a real ship, just
a kind of story one, but the Japanese have
unloaded it for years and years. It is supposed to bring them some good gift that they
didn't expect—prosperity, or courage, or patriotism, or something like that—to last them
all the year."

There was silence in the group for a moment,
and then Doris, who had been listening with
shining eyes to her brother, suddenly clapped
her hands. "I know what we can do," she
exclaimed. "It's never been done before and
there's plenty of time to plan it, for we have
a whole week." She rapidly unfolded the
scheme for their celebration of New Year's
Day to the interested boys and girls.

"It's splendid!"

"We can work in New Year's calls and New
Year's resolutions with it."

"Let's begin to-morrow. We can meet at
school during recess." The comments flew
thick and fast as Dr. Richards's class, the
banner class of the Sunday school, went out
into the street, and finally scattered to go home.

Hill Crest was trying to feel the holiday

spirit in spite of the fact that fathers, and uncles, and older brothers had been called during many preceding months to follow the colors. Windows were bright with holly and laurel wreaths, and through half-drawn curtains there could be seen the green and glitter of still standing Christmas trees. The town seemed strangely quiet though. There was always an eagerly anxious crowd waiting for the opening of the morning's mail at the post office, and the usual holiday party in Sunday school had been omitted.

Unexpectedly, however, a new, blither spirit seemed to pervade the town. The boys whistled, and the girls held merry conferences at the street corners. The meetings of Dr. Richards's class overflowed the day-school recess hour, and it met at the different houses, while the principal of the school was prevailed upon to give the boys the use of the manual training room after school. Hammers and saws and needles and thimbles were busy. The leftover holiday ribbons and bright paper that had wrapped packages were pressed and smoothed until they were fresh enough to use over again. Pens were busy in the work of writing letters and cards, and Dr. Richards, the Hill Crest rector, smiled as he looked out of the window of his study and saw the activities of his eager boys and girls. His little daughter, Doris, had taken him into her confidence and he had an inkling of what was going on.

"I knew they wouldn't fail me," he said. "Boys and girls like those, working together, can accomplish anything."

New Year's Eve came on the wings of a snow flurry. Just enough snow fell to make the roads beautiful and fine for sleighing. When the weather cleared and the eve itself was glorious with an early winter's sunset, and clear, frosty air, Hill Crest left its curtains up a little later than usual. Lamps were not lit, for everyone wanted to look out and watch the colors in the sky. The earth looked like a clean white page on which were illuminated the beauties of the sunset. Suddenly, though, a strange spectacle was seen coming down the street.

No one would have recognized Jack Newton's canoe, rigged up as it was with a sail made of sheeting, and mounted on a pair of sledge runners. It was draped with white cloth too, over which frost powder had been scattered, and from the bow flew the white flag of Japan with its big crimson ball and rays in the center. Boys drew this odd craft, and in it stood two quaint figures.

When Bruce and Doris had returned with

their father from his missionary post in Japan, they had brought some old ceremonial costumes which had been given them. Bruce stood in the bow of the boat, wearing a long brocaded robe over his reefer, and behind him was Doris with a bright kimona and sash covering her coat. These two had been chosen to man the craft, and Bruce held the Stars and Stripes high as they moved along. Following and crowding close to this treasure ship were the other boys and girls of the class, laughing, and their arms filled with packages.

The New Year's treasure ship stopped first at Professor Newton's house and Jack was delegated to present to his father, the school principal, a blank book that the girls had bound in soft gray leather, and in which as many as possible of the school children had written. Jack's own New Year's resolve headed the list:

I am going to plug at mathematics all the year.

YOUR SON.

Other good resolutions followed.

I am going to try not to be late for school for a term.

I shall try to have better marks in language.

I am going to pass next term.

It seemed to Professor Newton that a midyear in school had never opened so auspiciously as the one that was bound up in his treasure book.

"Thank you; good luck!" he called as the ship moved on down the street.

It stopped next at the Old Soldiers' Home. In the stress of selecting and sending away a division of young men these old veterans had been temporarily forgotten. Their home was almost as bare as a barracks, and the new year would open for them as only one march farther away from the old days of their gloriously remembered service for their country. But the New Year's treasure ship unloaded at the door of the Old Soldiers' Home a comforting kind of cargo. The boys and girls had gone without sweets for a week at home, and had brought the packages of sugar that their mothers had given them in return for their sacrifices. Each mother had added a package of tea, and there was a tiny American flag for each old veteran to wear in his buttonhole.

"To make you remember for a whole year how proud our town is of you," Bruce told them, "and we're coming over again to see you as often as we can."

It was the treasure of renewed friendship and patriotism that the ship left for the old soldiers.

Everyone in Hill Crest knew how brave
Mrs. Hildreth had been. She had given her
two boys for the colors, and her husband was
gone as an army surgeon. The builders of the
New Year's ship had wondered, and puzzled,
and schemed to try and think of something to
take the plucky little doctor's wife who sat
so many hours in the empty office, looking
down the road that led to the railway station.

"We haven't a thing for dear Mrs. Hildreth,"
Doris said. Bruce thought a moment.

"The post office isn't closed yet," he exclaimed. "Draw us down that way, boys, and
let's see if there's any mail for Mrs. Hildreth."

It was wonderful luck, but there was mail
for her. A fat letter with a foreign postmark
found its way into the treasure ship and on,
into the anxious mother's hands. She could
scarcely speak for joy. The letter told her
that her loved ones were safe and thinking
of her.

"That was the best New Year's treasure of
all, hope for Mrs. Hildreth, wasn't it?" Doris
said, softly, as they moved on again.

It was growing dusk now and the children
and their treasure ship looked like figures
from a story as they took their way through
the white streets. They stopped at Billy
Blake's house with a package of books. Billy

had been lame for years, and although everyone loved him for his pluck in pain, and for
his unfailing good cheer, the boys and girls
sometimes forgot him in their more active
work and play. But the package was made
up of one Christmas book from each boy and
girl in the class. They were the books too,
that they would have liked to keep, and the
best part of the gift was the note on top of
the package. It read:

DEAR BILLY:

One of us is coming every week for all the year to read
these books out loud to you.

It was not so much having Ivanhoe, and
Robinson Crusoe, and Green Mountain Boys
with pictures, and Scout books too, that made
Billy so happy, but the treasure that was his
in knowing that his boy and girl neighbors
were going to remember him as they never
had before through the coming year.

The Hill Crest grocery store was open.
Mr. Jones, who kept it, had to work late because he was short of help, and sometimes he
delivered after hours himself.

"Mr. Jones, O, Mr. Jones," the children
shouted in the door to him. "We've got
something for you." Jack handed the grocer,
whom they had all known since they were too

small to reach up to the counter, a legal looking
document that they had signed and sealed
with a red star.   He read it:

Resolved that all the boys and girls in our class are
going to carry home our groceries after this and save
Mr. Jones part of his work.

No wonder the grocer's smile was very
broad as he tucked the treasure that meant
time-saving for him the coming year into his
desk, and gave lollipops to each member of
the New Year's ship's crew.

"I am glad that we left father's surprise
until the last," Doris said.

"Let's leave the ship in Jack's barn now,"
Bruce suggested.   "Doris and I will fold up
these ceremonial togs and leave them in it
until to-morrow, and then we can all go around
to the rectory."

Hidden in their arms as they started were
the Red Cross banner and pledges for Junior
Red Cross work during the year that they
knew would please their rector more than any
other gift of treasure they could make him.
Their joy at giving these pledges of service,
for a year, and Dr. Richards's joy at receiving
them were overshadowed, though, in the surprise that awaited them.   Doris stood beside
her father in one end of the big rectory living

room, her cheeks pink with excitement, as she enjoyed her classmates' wonder. A huge log blazed in the fireplace, and the room was lighted with Japanese lanterns, Japanese flags were hung with the Stars and Stripes, and sweet-smelling joss sticks burned in vases. There were tops to spin, Japanese water flowers to watch unfold in bowls of water, the town librarian had come to tell the class quaint stories of that far-away land, and there was a simple feast of rice cakes and tea.

When the fun of this unexpected party was over, Dr. Richards spoke to them:

"I know that the boys and girls of my banner class feel that the new year will break for them in a happier way than ever before," he said. "We have much to learn from the customs of the Old World, and especially this year, when we ought to look for the kind of gifts the treasure ship brings—comfort, and hope, and help for those who need it."

"For all the year too," Doris said. And the boys and girls, in imagination, could see their treasure ship anchored somewhere near Hill Crest from one New Year's Day to the next—its cargo made up of the treasures of service, and neighborliness, and help.

HOW THEY FOUND LINCOLN

THE Lincoln's Birthday celebration was going to be held in old Mr. Baxter's house. There couldn't possibly be a better place for it, the boys and girls of the neighborhood thought, for Mr. Baxter had seen Lincoln.

Rainy Saturdays the old veteran would let a few of them sit beside the fire in his cozy sitting room as he told them stories of their martyred President. The walls were hung with old flags that had been new in Lincoln's time, and Mr. Baxter's sword stood in one corner back of the stove. There was a painting of Lincoln hanging above the mantelpiece, and the haircloth chairs and the table covered with green baize had been used in the time of the Civil War.

"He was a plain man," Mr. Baxter would begin the story he loved to tell about Lincoln, "with not any of the schooling that you youngsters have to-day. He was raised to do farm work, and he bought his best suit of clothes by splitting rails to pay for it. He learned to write on flat logs, and in the snow, and on his wooden shovel. But Abraham Lincoln had enough power and heart to carry our country

128

through her greatest danger, and keep her the United States."

Then Mr. Baxter would hobble over to his chest of drawers and get out his treasures; his Grand Army uniform and badge, a yellowed newspaper that told of the death of Lincoln, a copy of the Emancipation Proclamation, and the badge of his regiment.

They were always new and exciting to Hal and Priscilla, and Frederick, and the others. It had been Frederick who thought of the celebration for Lincoln's Birthday.

"We want to get up some kind of an entertainment for February twelfth, Mr. Baxter," he had said a fortnight before. "We thought we could all do things to make us remember Mr. Lincoln, and ask the mothers and fathers to come."

"Fine!" old Mr. Baxter had said, chuckling, and pounding the rag carpet with his cane. "And you can celebrate right here in this room, with the grown folks out in the kitchen to look in at you."

The plan had grown as the boys and girls talked it over at home and after school.

"We'll read everything we can about Lincoln," Priscilla said one day on the way home from school, "and then plan charades and pantomimes and things to learn and recite."

"You and Hal ought to have the best parts," Frederick said, "because your father is the head of the town historical society."

"Well, your father gave the school library, Frederick," Hal broke in. "I think you deserve to begin the program. Here we are at the grocery store, and mother wanted us to order some things. O, hello, Phil." Hal's voice changed to a patronizing tone as he leaned across the counter and spoke to a boy behind it. "Send us over five pounds of sugar and a dozen eggs, will you?"

"All right, Hal," and the boy's face, that had lighted to see his schoolmates, flushed. Then he took courage and called to them as the three started out of the door. "O, Hal, I heard about the entertainment you're going to have out at Mr. Baxter's. Maybe I could get off to come. I'd like to. There isn't anything I could do in it, is there?"

"No, I don't think so," Frederick said, quickly. "It's about all planned now. We'll need somebody to help bring over benches from the school though. You could help with that, maybe."

Phil bent over the sugar barrel so that the boys wouldn't see the deeper flush that covered his face. In a second he looked up, and spoke bravely.

"All right; I'll try to be on hand to bring benches," he said.

At their gate Priscilla spoke, just as Frederick went on toward his house.

"Maybe we ought to have planned a part for Phil in the entertainment. Mr. Baxter says that Lincoln was a poor boy and had to work, and Phil did look so disappointed."

"That's just like a girl," Frederick said.

"We can't change things now, Priscilla. It's all planned," Hal decided.

Such excitement as there was the days before the eventful one of Lincoln's Birthday! Mr. Baxter decided to give one of his old flags that had been carried in Lincoln's time to the boy or girl who honored the great man best at the entertainment. The library was searched for books that would help, attics were ransacked for old costumes, and every child was so busy that the twelfth came before they knew it.

Phil had watched the boys and girls go by the store, their eager voices coming in to him as he measured potatoes and flour, or took off his apron to shoulder a basket and deliver groceries. Since he had been old enough to help his father with the store, and in this way save the wages of a clerk, Phil had felt shut out of his schoolmates' games. He had little time for play. He opened the store and swept it before school in the morning. After school and all day Saturday he was either filling orders over the counter or calling at his school-mates' back doors with groceries.

"They don't want me in their fun," Phil thought, as he watched the whole town prepare for Lincoln's Birthday with flying flags and red, white, and blue bunting.

Old Mr. Baxter was as excited as the boys and girls over the entertainment. As he polished his sword and helped arrange the benches that the school janitor brought over to his big sunny kitchen, he felt young again. He could hear in fancy the drum call and the bugles of long ago. He could see a tall dark man, ungainly, but with the kindest face in the world, standing on the steps of the White House. He heard again Lincoln's words, "I do order and declare that all persons held as slaves shall be free."

Everything was ready at last. It was the afternoon of the great day. Mr. Baxter put on his Grand Army uniform and opened the white front door to let in the fathers and mothers, and the children.

The boys and girls gathered in the back hall, getting in line for their part in the celebration. Priscilla peeped through into the kitchen.

"There's a whole crowd of people here, sitting on the benches," she whispered. "They can see into the sitting room nicely. Mr. Baxter is finding places for them, and going around talking to them. Phil isn't there though."

"I guess he didn't want to do anything to help after all," Hal said. "Well, I suppose we had better begin. It's your turn first, Priscilla."

Priscilla looked very winsome indeed as she stepped into the winter sunshine that flooded Mr. Baxter's sitting room. In her short flowered dress, black lace mitts, and wide rimmed hat she seemed a part of the old days when Lincoln had lived and worked in just such a room. Without a break she recited the words a great poet wrote in memory of Lincoln.

"O Captain! my Captain! rise up and hear the bells;
  Rise up—for you the flag is flung—for you the bugle trills."

Then Frederick, dressed in woodsman's clothes, came in and split rails in pantomime. Hal, dressed in a homespun suit and fur cap, was seen poring over the life of Washington, Lincoln's first book. The other children did their parts; one played "Old Black Joe" on a violin; four sang "America," and one boy recited the whole of Lincoln's Emancipation Proclamation.

And as each, in turn, had their share in the applause, they looked longingly at the faded Stars and Stripes of an old battlefield with which Mr. Baxter had draped Lincoln's picture. That was to be the prize for the boy or girl who had shown best what Lincoln's Birthday means for to-day.

They had all finished at last. The sunlight had faded, and Mr. Baxter stood in the fading glow of the room, facing the mothers and fathers. In his old blue uniform he was truly a soldier of Lincoln, ready to give them a message from the great captain. He touched the folds of the flag and was about to speak when the door opened, and there was a stir among the children who had grouped themselves around him. They tried to push the breathless boy back, but Phil pressed through. He wore his working clothes, and his hands were stained from measuring vegetables. He did not seem to notice the company or to think of anything except his need to reach Mr. Baxter and speak to him.

"What do you want? There isn't any place for you here," the children whispered to Phil, but Mr. Baxter reached out a kind hand to the boy and drew him to his side.

"What is it, lad?" he asked. Phil opened his hand in which was clasped a nickel.

"You came in to buy some tea this morning, Mr. Baxter," he said. "I was so busy, and father wasn't there to help me; that's the reason I made a mistake in your change. I took five cents too much. I found it out when I counted the money in the cash drawer. and I ran all the way here to give it to you. I wanted to come this morning and help move in the benches, but I couldn't leave my work." Phil paused; then, looking at all the people in front of him, he shrank back.

There was a murmur of pleasure among the mothers and fathers at Phil's honest words. He had seemed like part of the entertainment, coming in so suddenly.

Mr. Baxter drew him forward and spoke.

"A long time ago there was another lad who worked in a grocery store," he said. "He had to work just as hard as Phil does, and at night when the store was locked, he used to get out a few books that he had saved his money to buy, and study them by the light of the candle. One day he too made a mistake in giving change. He knew that he must make it right, and although it was pitch dark, and three miles that he had to tramp through the woods to give back the pennies to a woman, he did it.

"Then this boy grew up, and they made him President of the United States, and he did the greatest thing in our history, he kept the States united. But what everybody loved to call him, more than President even, was—" Mr. Baxter waited a second, and the children finished for him:

"Honest Abe," they said.

"Yes, that was just it," Mr. Baxter said as he turned to the picture of Lincoln and took down the flag. He held it up so that the Stars and Stripes caught the last of the sunset light.

"Which of you deserves this flag?" he asked. "I want it to belong to the child who has kept this Lincoln's Birthday best, and I think I'll let you boys and girls decide."

There was hardly a moment's silence, and it was Frederick who broke it.

"Honest Phil!" he said.

"Yes, Phil ought to have it," the others agreed.

Phil couldn't speak he was so happy. He held the beautiful old colors close to him as the children crowded around him, a new comradeship in their kind looks and friendly words.

Then came the mothers' and fathers' surprise, a patriotic supper for Mr. Baxter and the boys and girls. There were ham and tongue sandwiches piled on plates and topped by little flags, rosy apples, white-frosted cakes, and red and white peppermint sticks. Phil helped to serve the good things. When every crumb was gone, they all sang "The Star-Spangled Banner" as Phil held the old flag high above his head.

It had been a splendid Lincoln's Birthday, they decided. On the way home Phil said that he wanted to take the flag to school and keep it there so it would really belong to them all. Left alone, old Mr. Baxter lighted a lamp and held it up so that it shone straight into the kind, plain face of Lincoln in the picture.

"I'm glad the children know you too now," he said. "I wanted them to know you as we did, and the little grocer's boy helped me." You sat in the White House, and you were the captain of our country, but first, and always, and last you were our Honest Abe."

WHEN SAINT VALENTINE CROSSED SCHOONER BAY

"NOT much of a chance of our getting any valentines this year," Billy Mack said, a frown puckering his forehead as he looked out of the tiny panes of the window of the cabin. A fire burned briskly in the sheet-iron stove inside, there was the odor of crisp loaves baking in the oven, and the kitchen-sitting-and-dining room in one was comfortable with some of the furnishings they had brought from home; but it was Labrador for all that.

Mother, father, Billy, and Nancy Mack lived in a cabin on Schooner Bay. Father was the only doctor in the scattered neighborhood for miles around. Just across the Bay was the hospital. Dr. Mack crossed on the ice two or three times a week to set broken legs and treat frozen hands and ears, and cure more than one case of pneumonia. Cruel weather it was, such as only Labrador knows when the winter and the spring are contending with each other. There had been a mild spell, when a splashing warm rain came down in a melting drizzle. The cliffs dripped as if they

were promising spring flowers, and the road
that led from the cabin to the edge of the Bay
was full of slush. Then there had been a shift
in the weather and everything was frozen stiff
again overnight; but the whole, white sweep of
the ice, that was as heavy as a beamed flooring
for the dog sleds, was shivering underneath
the currents of the Bay, and trying to break
away, urged by the wind blowing briskly out
to sea.

"The post won't be here for a week yet in
this weather," Billy's mother said, turning away
from the oven of bread as the boy spoke.
"Perhaps when it does come it will bring you
a valentine or two from the city."

"Well, we've our valentines of last year,
and the year before, and the year before that,"
Nancy said, opening a box that she had brought
into the room. "We can play that they just
came, Billy, and that Saint Valentine found
us, after all, even 'way up here in Labrador."

"So we can," Billy cried, and the brother
and sister poured out the bright contents of
the box on the table. Filmy lace paper, and
gilt and silver doves, bright scarlet hearts and
daintily inscribed messages of friendship all
reminded the children of the days when the
postman had brought these letters of love to
the door by hand, not by sled over fields of ice.

"O, but they're pretty, aren't they?" Nancy exclaimed.

"Here's the valentine that grandmother sent," Billy said, opening a folded piece of paper at the top of which two doves were beautifully drawn in pen and ink. "She made it all herself," he said, and he read the writing aloud:

"This is the day, February fourteenth, when we try to be kind to every one. We wish to give, not only loving thoughts and words, but deeds to our friends, because it is a day set for kind feeling—"

"Dear grandmother," Nancy said, softly. Then she added: "Granny Thomas is over at the hospital at the Cove. Father said she was laid up with rheumatism."

"And Skipper Brisk's little lad, Peter, is in the hospital too, getting his lame leg straightened out."

For a minute the two children were quiet, fingering their precious store of valentines. When Nancy spoke she said exactly what was in Billy's mind: "I think Granny Thomas and Peter would each like to have a valentine."

As if he had already planned a way to cross to the hospital whose white roof could just be seen across Schooner Bay at the Cove, Billy added, "The dog team's fine and fresh, for the dogs didn't go out yesterday, and father won't need them until to-morrow."

"Yes, we'll go," Nancy decided.

When they told their mother of their plan she was a little worried. "The wind is from the south," she said, "and you know what that means—there'll be a break-up soon."

"The ice will hold together in the Bay for many a day yet," their father said. "You mustn't set too much store in these early frosts. Billy's as good a driver as I am, and he and Nancy will easily be able to get over to the Cove with their valentines, and back. I would go too, but there's too much sickness on this side of the Bay for me to be able to leave to-day."

The dogs, little wolflike creatures, were glad to be off. They pulled the long, low sled in individual traces, and it took only a little while to harness them. In the warm comfort of the fur rugs that lined the sled Nancy was cuddled with the box of valentines in her lap. Billy ran along beside the dogs, urging and guiding them. He was bundled in furs too, and both children were as warm as toast. They soon left the trail of the road, and the dogs, with long, loping strides, struck out on to the wide, white ice sheet of Schooner Bay.

"I guess Skipper Brisk's little lad, Peter,

ought to have two or three valentines. We've
plenty to go around," Nancy said from the
depths of her rugs. "O, Billy, isn't it wonderful out here—so far away from everything, and
so still!" she exclaimed after a while.

"I wish it *wasn't* so still," Billy said, as he
seated himself on the sled beside her. The
dogs knew the way now and were trudging
steadily on, with little need of driving. "The
sun's gone under and the wind feels wet, like
snow," he said, a little fearfully.

The boy was right in his prophecy. The
weather changed as quickly as it often does
in that strange northerly place; a storm was
on them. The gray sky, so shortly before
a vivid blue, thickened to drab and then to
black. A sudden puff of southerly wind
brought the wet snow, and then the rain.
Although it was barely dusk, because of the
almost limitless spaces of the Bay they lost
sight of the track across the Cove. No man
could have found his way; only dogs could
find the track through such a gale.

Billy folded the robes more closely around
Nancy. "Don't be afraid," he urged, trying,
in comforting her, to still his own fright.
"The team's been across a hundred times this
winter and the dogs know every inch of the
way."

"I'm trying to be brave," Nancy replied, her voice scarcely carrying above the wind. "And the box of valentines is all right. I have it well wrapped up here in the robes."

After their first terror at the darkness that had settled down so suddenly, the children began to enjoy their race with the storm. The dogs, trotting briskly along, were warm. The children, themselves, so warmly wrapped up, were flushed and comfortable. After an hour's driving, the rain slackened, although the wind still hurried along with them from the south. Then the sky cleared and with it came the sight of the long, straight road across the ice to the Cove that the dogs had not left for a minute.

"There's the hospital; why, we're almost there," Nancy shouted. Whatever Billy would have said in reply was stopped by a sudden noise. A shrill crack it was at first; then it deepened to a boom like that of far-away thunder, coming nearer, though, and broken by a series of sharp cracks that surrounded the sled and the dog team. The ice felt, beneath the children, as if it were a giant piece of paper crumpling to pieces. It was breaking up in Schooner Bay, sooner than anybody had expected, because of the early warm spell and the rain. The wind whimpered, and pushed, and helped to split it as it broke. When a sudden ray of sunshine broke through the sky, the children could see plainly what a plight they were in.

When the ice goes out it breaks into great pans that float along over the top of the water like shining, white rafts. Billy and Nancy, and the sled and the dogs were in the middle of a good-sized pan now. All around them was swirling water, foaming white at being so suddenly released.

Nancy sobbed a little, but she soon stopped, for an idea had put courage into her heart. "Maybe mother'll see the break-up from the shore and fetch father to send for us in Skipper Brisk's skiff," she said.

"They'll have to hurry though," Billy said. He wet his finger and held it up to feel the wind. Then his face went white as he saw the friendly curve of the Cove shore receding from sight. "We're going away from the Cove," he said. "We're going out to sea."

The dogs huddled together and snarled viciously, their wolf instincts roused by the danger. Billy tried to distract their attention by feeding them some meat he had brought with him. It kept them quiet and prevented their overturning the sled into the water. Then he tried to think. Whatever was done, he must do. It was his work to save his sister's life, if he could. The pan of ice upon which they were marooned was almost the only one that was floating out to sea. The others, some of which were quite as large, were going toward the shore. If only one of these pans would come near enough, he thought, they could step across to it, that is, if it touched their pan. Then another adventuresome thought came to him. Why not try to pull up alongside a pan that was floating in the opposite direction?

The cold, weighted as it was with the dampness from the water, was bitter now. To work, Billy had to take off his fur mittens, and he pulled Nancy from her rugs and told her what she too must do with her bare hands to help him. Their fingers stiffened, but they would not feel their ache as they unharnessed the dogs, who, let loose, bounded and pawed about them, getting in the way and making their task twice as hard. The long, thin tendons of skin that had made the dogs' traces they cut with Billy's knife. Then they spliced them to make a coil with a lasso loop in the end.

"Put your arms as tight as you can around my waist, Nancy," Billy said as he held the coiled lasso tightly over his shoulder, and planted his feet firmly on the ice. "I must wait until I see a pan that's floating in to the shore, and it must have a jagged piece to throw this lasso around. When I throw, hold me fast or I'll slip into the water."

It seemed hours instead of seconds that they waited. The quickly tacking wind and the currents of the Bay made the pans float in every direction; now several would almost touch, then they would be so widely separated as to leave a great sweep of open water.

Billy watched for his chance. Soon it came, a big, round pan with a ragged spar of ice sticking up at one end where it had splintered. It was within throwing distance. Billy twisted the lasso over his head.

"Hold fast, Nancy," he begged between his clinched teeth. Then he threw.

As straight as he had aimed the lasso cut through the air, catching and tightening around the ice spar that looked like a rudder on the end of the pan. His feet slipped as he pulled, but Nancy held him pluckily, and they both braced themselves, heels dug into the ice, for the long, hard pull. The lasso cut the boy's hands; at first the force of the weight of their pan pulled the other out of its shoreward course. It seemed as if both pans would drift out to sea, but slowly, the strong pulling of the

skin tendon drew the other alongside. The
dogs leaped over. Billy followed, and reached
his hand out to help Nancy, who had gone
back for the treasure box of valentines and
was just in time to cross before the two pans
drifted apart.

In the center of the new pan, their sled gone,
Billy and Nancy clung to each other and the
dogs whined at their feet. The pan had changed
its course a little with the pulling. Would it
resume its old course, they wondered? Slowly,
though, it turned. Now it was drifting toward
the Cove, and the water was quite free of
ice and settling down into a quiet, blue calm.
They were away from the treacherous ice field
now. Suddenly, like the wings of a messenger
dove in the distance, floating between the Cove
and them, Billy and Nancy saw the sails of
Skipper Brisk's skiff bearing down to rescue
them.

There never was such a Saint Valentine's
Day at the Cove hospital. There was the
patients' loved doctor, who had come so unexpectedly in the skiff, and Billy and Nancy
were there with so many valentines that every
one had three or four apiece. Skipper Brisk's
little lad, Peter, sat up in bed and shared his
supper with his daddy who came so unexpectedly, when no one supposed the skiff would be able

to sail for six weeks or so. Granny Thomas sat up in bed too, and as she smiled down on her lapful of red hearts she said, "Not even the breakup stopped them.   Saint Valentine crossed Schooner Bay!"

THE SLACKER

THEODORE shrank into the corner of the school lunch room as he opened the basket that his grandmother had packed so carefully for him. It was a good feast, for a hungry boy at recess, even if the others did jeer at it: a couple of cold, rich sausages, rye bread spread thickly with butter and jam, and a ring of frosted coffee cake. Theodore bit hastily into it, a sausage in one hand and a slice of bread and jam in the other. Perhaps, he thought, if he hurried, no one would make fun of his queer food.

A crowd of boys bore down on him now though. Theodore slipped his lunch basket behind him and almost choked, his fair face flushing up to the roots of his thick mop of yellow hair. But the boys had not noticed that he was eating. It was something else they had come about.

"Hello, Dutchy!" In spite of the nickname, Theodore thought that he could detect a new note of comradeship in his classmates' voices. He looked up, his face glowing with pleasure instead of mortification.

"Hello!" he answered.

The others plunged right into facts.

"We're starting a new club, Dutchy," they explained. "It's going to be a patriotic club, the Junior Reserve. The gymnasium instructor belongs to the Home Guard, you know, and he's going to drill us. We're going to save up and buy a new flag for the school for Washington's Birthday, and we'll get uniforms for ourselves, white and blue, like sailors. You can belong to our Junior Reserve, Dutchy, if you like," they finished, generously.

A second's silence followed in which no one spoke. Theodore had felt, first hot, and then faint.

"Well, didn't you hear us?" the others asked at last.

"Sure, I heard," it was all Theodore could say.

"Aren't you going to join?" they gasped, finally.

"No," Theodore replied.

He thought, at first, that the whole eager, young-American crowd of them was going to fall on him tooth and nail. He stood up and braced himself against the brick wall, putting his fist up to save his head; but they didn't touch him. He wished, then, that they had, for what they did was worse. The boys turned and left him, muttering, "Slacker," every one of them, in their scorn.

After school was out Theodore heard it over and over again. He lived next to the school. His grandfather kept a shop, half for toys and sweets, and half for school supplies such as pads and pencils and pencil boxes. Theodore had to shovel the snow from the sidewalk when he went home, and then wait upon customers while his grandfather and grandmother had their afternoon cup of coffee in the cozy little dining room back of the store. As he cleaned the sidewalk Theodore heard taunting voices from behind fences and trees. Then a boy opened the shop door, and called in at Theodore behind the counter, running out noisily and slamming the door behind him.

"Slacker!" That was what they all called him. It brought tears of shame to his eyes.

Theodore's grandfather went soundly asleep in his chair, and snored after his coffee, and his grandmother got out her knitting and sat down with it beside the fire. Theodore could very well tend the store, for there was nothing to do. There were no customers. Hardly anyone had bought anything in his grandfather's store for as long as a year now. The children went downtown to the toy and stationery department of the general store. It seemed too bad, Theodore thought, as he looked over the stock and covered it for the night.

There was a gross of new lead pencils, not opened, that they had put into stock a month before. His grandfather had particularly liked them, for they had red, white, and blue papers about the wood. There were the neat little pencil boxes, too, that Theodore's grandfather had carved. He had been a very clever toy-maker on the edge of the Black Forest in his young days, and no other woodworker for miles around could carve so swiftly or so well as he. It had been his pleasure to bring his art with him to America and put quaint, handmade toys for sale in his shop, at low prices that boys and girls could pay.

He had carved those pencil boxes. There was a little raised star on the end of each for pulling out the cover; there was an American flag cut in the cover and colored. But none of the children had come in to buy one of the patriotic pencil boxes.

Theodore leaned on the window sill of the shop now, and looked out at the bare trees and the snow-covered ground. Winter was always the pleasantest time for him; his grand-parents tried to give him all the happiness then that had been theirs in their childhood. For weeks before they three collected bright balls, and gold and silver cobwebs for the little green Christmas tree. His grandmother made gingerbread horses and gnomes, and they gilded nuts for it too, and it was lighted for many nights after Christmas. But on the tip top of Theodore's tree they always put a small American flag.

When his grandfather played "Tannenbaum" on his old fiddle of a winter's evening, he always followed it with "America." A picture of George Washington hung on the wall, and once in a while the old man would take down a tin box from the shelf in the kitchen and unlock it, and show Theodore the gold pieces inside—not many, but a growing pile.

"To send you to college, boy, he would chuckle. "To make you into a fine American citizen."

Remembering it all, Theodore felt as if he couldn't stand the days that would follow. He wanted to belong to the Junior Reserve. He wasn't a slacker, but he couldn't ask his grandfather for money to buy a uniform. The store rent had to be paid, and there was no money coming in. He simply could not ask his grandfather for any of the gold pieces locked up in the tin box.

It was dark now in the shop; there was no sound but the click of his grandmother's knitting needles, as she seamed his new woolen stockings. They were both so good to him, and there didn't seem to be anything that he could do for his grandparents, Theodore thought. He put his head down in his arms and tried to keep back his sobs.

The days that followed were hard for Theodore. He found notes with "Slacker" written in them on his desk at school. All the boys avoided him, and he was so lonesome that it hurt. He stood on the curbing and watched the Junior Reserve drill in their natty new uniforms; not an eye turned toward him though. It was just as if his classmates did not know him. The Junior Reserve had a fife-and-drum corps too. The day before Washington's Birthday they brought their new flag to the school. The fife-and-drum corps marched first; then four boys marched, holding Old Glory out wide, by the four corners. It was a very great occasion indeed, and the climax came when the principal said that the flag should hang out of the window of the Seventh Grade, the Junior Reserve's and Theodore's class.

The morning of Washington's Birthday Theodore went down to school to clean erasers. He leaned out of the window, beating them together; there was the flag, its stars and stripes gleaming just below him. He reached down and touched its folds with a reverent hand.

"Don't you dare touch that! It isn't your flag; it's ours," came shrilly up to him from the schoolyard where the Junior Reserve was drilling.

Theodore drew back, cringing. At that moment a blast of a February gale blew round the corner of the schoolhouse. It whipped and lashed the flag; then it suddenly stripped it from its hooks, which had been a poor fastening at best for it. The wind carried it up and down, and played with it a moment. Then it left it on a high branch of a bare old tree at the farther end of the school playground. It was at the mercy of a rough day.

Theodore finished cleaning his erasers and then went down and out into the school grounds. A group of boys were gathered underneath the tree and he could hear what they said.

"Too bad."

"We'll have to get another flag."

"Nobody could get the flag out of that tree; the limb it's caught on is dead!"

Then they went back to their drilling again.

When there was no one to notice him, Theodore went over to the tree and looked up at the flag. It was torn some already; after a night of that wind it would be in ribbons.

What a pity, he thought, that not one of the boys had tried to get it. A dead limb, they said, but perhaps they didn't know. It might not be dead, and if it were, it still might hold a twelve-year-old boy's weight. Theodore looked behind him. Not a boy was looking at the flag. They did not seem to be thinking of it. He began climbing the tree.

The limb around which the flag was twisted grew at a good distance up the trunk of the tree. Then it stretched straight out, a dizzy length from the tree, smooth, slippery with ice, and tapering at the end. It was a different color from the rest of the limbs, grayish, where they were brown. Theodore climbed up the trunk safely, but as he started out on the limb, working his way along as an animal does, it not only bent with him; it crackled.

Theodore did not allow himself to look down at the ground; it was a long distance below him. On he went, clinging, crawling, the colors of the flag gleaming as a kind of beacon light for his courage, for the limb was bending more than was safe. There was another branch below that he might be able to catch if he fell, but he knew he must reach the flag first.

A confused murmur of voices from below him came up to Theodore now and made his feat more difficult.

"It's Dutchy—after the flag!"

"He'll never get it; the limb's breaking now."

"He'll be killed."

"Well, what if it does break?" he thought at last. He had the flag now. Clinging with one hand, he unwound it cautiously with the other. Then he slipped it over his shoulder and started back along the limb, but it was too weak for him now. Crash, crack! There was the next branch down left. Theodore caught hold of it in falling, but it was too slippery for him to be able to get any kind of grip on it.

"I don't care how hard I hit; I've brought the flag back safe," was Theodore's last thought as he plunged down, toward the ground—and into the arms of the Junior Reserve who had made a human net to catch him.

He was a little dazed at first, especially when they told him how brave they thought he was, but he soon got over that. They carried him all the way home so that they might stand around him while he told his grandfather the fine news, that he was to be flag bearer for the Junior Reserve. And it was worth it all, to see how glad Theodore's grandfather was. He got out his fiddle and played "America" for them, and then he insisted upon opening the package of red, white, and blue pencils and giving each boy one. They bought pencil boxes, and they gave Theodore three cheers when they went home.

"A flag-bearer, eh, lad?" his grandfather said after they had gone. "Chosen on the birthday of our new country's father! And now for a uniform, maybe, like the others?"

"O, yes, please," Theodore said, looking at the empty place where the pencil boxes had stood.

SAINT PATRICK'S DAY IN THE MORNING

"STIR yourself, Patsy, my boy, and get your schoolbooks together. It's near eight-thirty," Mrs. Murphy warned, looking up from the foaming tub in the kitchen where she was washing, and over to the boy by the window.

"I know it, mother. Haven't I been watching the clock ever since seven and wishing the hands would stand still?" he answered with a frown that seemed quite out of place on his merry, freckled face.

"Why, Patsy, lad!" his mother stopped rubbing, a look of what seemed like fear coming over her face as she glanced at the calendar that hung on the wall and then again searchingly at Patsy. "What should you be dreading school for to-day, with you at the head of your class, and the teacher telling me you'll pass with honors into the next?"

"You know what day it is," the boy said, doggedly.

"The grandest day in all Ireland," his mother said, "Saint Patrick's Day! Can't I shut my eyes and see it all when I was a girl on your

159

grandfather's farm in the old country? We'd
be getting ready for the day for weeks, saving
our bits of finery to wear to the party they'd
be giving in the town hall, and doing as much
work as we could beforehand so as to have
plenty of time to sing and make merry. I can
hear the music of the harps too. Those were
grand days, son."

"But they were days in Ireland, mother,"
Patsy said, "and this is America. Nobody
here seems to think much of Saint Patrick's
Day except as a time for making sport of
Irish lads like me. The shops are full of green
badges, and hats, and clay pipes tied with
green, and shamrock plants. O, I heard the
boys talking at recess yesterday about what
they were going to do to me to-day. They're
going to throw potatoes at me outside in the
schoolyard, and tie my desk up with green
cloth so I'll be ashamed coming down from
assembly. I don't want to go to school to-day.
Let me stay home and help hang out the wash,
and carry home yesterday's ironing, mother.
You could write me an excuse and say that
you needed me," he begged.

"You're not afraid? O, Patsy, don't let me
think you're a coward. This is the day for
brave hearts in the old country, just as Washington's Birthday is the brave holiday in

America. We oughtn't to forget our own
strong men now that we're here in a strange
land. We ought to show America that we
can be brave too. Look, Patsy, here's a sign
for you. There's no shamrock in any shop
in town like ours."

Mrs. Murphy went over to the window and
broke off a sprig from the pot of green there.
Then, pinning it to the boy's jacket, "Wear
it Patsy," she begged, "for a mark of your
Irish pluck, and go along to school like a fine
son of Erin who's not afraid of a thing in the
world."

It seemed as if the tiny green leaves worked
a sudden charm in Patsy's heart. He straightened a bit, a merry smile came over his sober
face, and he put his hand on his mother's bent
shoulder.

"All right," he assented. He took his cap
down from the wall, picked up his books, and
opened the kitchen door. "Here's to Saint
Patrick's Day in the morning," he laughed,
"and whatever's coming to me because of my
wearing of the green."

Patsy was just in time for the last bell.
A flying potato, sent with good aim from the
corner of the schoolyard, hit him, but he
ducked a second one and got inside the hall
safely. He hung up his cap, and found that

the drum it was his duty to beat for the grades
on his floor to march up to assembly had been
decorated with a bow of green ribbon.

"I'll keep the green on," Patsy said to himself as he slung the drum strap over his shoulder
and took his place in the hall. "I'm going to
be proud of Erin's color to-day, and show it
beside my country's flag." He carried out
his thought as he took his place in the hall
next the great American flag that hung there,
and beat his drum for the boys and girls to
file out of their classroom and up the stairs
to the assembly hall.

In spite of the rule against whispering, there
were murmurs of ridicule as the long lines passed
Patsy. The boys had thought that he would,
of course, strip the green off his drum; instead
he was displaying it with evident pride. They
snickered, and the girls giggled openly, but
Patsy paid not the slightest attention to them.
He did not stop drumming until all had gone
upstairs. Then he followed, leaving his drum
at the door of the assembly room ready for the
end of the exercises.

Ordinarily, the assembly period, with its
readings, singing, and address by the school
principal, seemed long to Patsy. He was always
anxious to have it over so that he could get
down to his classroom and the lessons of which

he was so fond. But to-day the period seemed to pass too quickly. Patsy was a sensitive boy; he dreaded the jokes that might be waiting for him downstairs. He wished that the principal would touch upon the meaning of the day, and make the boys and girls feel, as his mother had made him feel, the glory of Ireland's old patriotism. But other matters had to be spoken of, and before Patsy realized it, they were singing the last verse of "America," and he slipped out to get his drum to be ready by the instant that they struck the last note. As he did so he noticed that the corner of the hall where he stood smelled of smoke.

"The janitor's built a fresh fire," he thought. "The day's very cold and windy."

As he took up his drumsticks, he saw a gray cloud sifting out of the cracks in the wall where the chimney was.

"The flue is dusty, I guess," he explained to himself.

But as the well-drilled line of grades marched out of the assembly room and began going down the stairs, Patsy realized that it was neither the odor of a freshly built fire that he smelled, or dust that he saw. The March winds had fanned the defective flue into a flame. The schoolhouse was on fire. Patsy stood in the heat and smoke of it, and he knew that he must stay there until every boy and girl was safely downstairs.

"They mustn't know," he said to himself. "The teachers have gone down by the back staircase, and as soon as they find out about the fire they can open the doors and let the classes right out. I'll beat faster, gradually, so the kids won't know that it's the fire drill march all at once. That would scare them, and they might run down the stairs, because the bell didn't ring for fire drill."

These thoughts flashed through Patsy's mind as he played his drum steadily, and without missing a single beat. He quickened the time, and the children marched faster. Short puffs of smoke were bursting out of the walls now, but the end of the line was nearing. It was made up of the grammar-grade boys who had discovered the fire, but were keeping their places well in line, realizing the danger of a panic.

Other thoughts began to crowd themselves now upon Patsy. The smoke had begun to choke him, and a sudden licking flame had scorched his hand. He beat on, but he felt dazed, and it seemed to him as if the scene were changing. The line passing down the stairs seemed to him an army of soldiers,

tramping between green fields. He could hear
the sound of harps, as his mother had said that
she had heard them, and he was warm with
the sun of Ireland's bright skies shining down
on him as he led this line of troops. He heard
a voice that seemed to come from a very long
distance speaking to him.

"Saint Patrick's Day in the morning—the
day of brave hearts, Here's shamrock for a
sign. Look, Patsy—"

Well, the last was a real voice anyway.
Patsy opened his eyes with a great effort and
found himself out in the schoolyard, in the
arms of a big Irish fireman. The man touched
the bit of shamrock, withered by the heat
now, but still pinned to Patsy's coat. A
crowd of kind, admiring schoolmates and
teachers surrounded them, and the fireman
spoke again.

"That's it; look up, lad! You're all right.
You drummed the lads and lassics out in
safety, and the fire's out now, with very little
damage. You're a plucky boy. Here's shamrock for a sign—on this day of brave hearts."

It was quite true. One of the teachers had
discovered the source of the fire in the chimney
and had sent in an alarm. Half of the children
had not known of it until the principal had
met them at the foot of the stairs and led them

out into the yard. The worst of it, heat and smoke combined, had been in the corner of the upper hall where Patsy had stuck to his post and drummed until the last boy was downstairs, and he, himself, had to be carried down by a fireman, where the pure air revived him. He felt as fresh as ever when ʾe heard the rousing cheers they gave him.

"Then they gave me the drum again," he told his mother proudly as they sat together at supper that night. "It was trimmed up with green, you know, still. And the music teacher took his pitch pipe out of his pocket and gave the key, and we all sang 'The Wearing of the Green' out there in the schoolyard as I played the drum for them. Wasn't it fine how they carried me home down the street, just as if I was a hero coming from the war, mother?"

"And why shouldn't they, lad?" Mrs. Murphy said with a twinkle in her eye. "Aren't you Irish, Patsy, and wasn't it Saint Patrick's Day in the morning? Now have another potato, son. There's nothing like a hot potato, unless it's a little sprig of shamrock, for putting a brave heart into one."

TERRENCE—APRIL FOOL

"WHO shall it be?" Bruce Hadley asked of the boys gathered outside of the school door. "There isn't any fun in fooling a boy who expects it and is going to be ready for anything we do to him. It's one big chance in a year and we ought to make the most of it."

There was a moment's silence as the others thought. Then Teddy Blake broke it. "I know; let's make an April fool of Terrence," he said.

As the words slipped out, a little girl came out of the door and paused a second on the edge of the group.

"Our April girl," Joan's father, the principal of the school, called her. Joan's eyes were as blue as the skies of April, and her hair was like strands of sunbeams. She was like her birth month, quick to smiles, and as quick to tears. Joan loved the whole world, and was sorry for every stray animal, or fallen bird, or neglected flower she saw. A flush of surprise made her cheeks pink as she caught Teddy's words.

"That's it; we'll give Terrence an April Fool's Day that he won't forget for the rest of the year," Bruce laughed, slapping Teddy's back in appreciation. Then half-whispered words passed back and forth between the other boys:

"Candy with pepper in it?"

"Hide his test papers?"

"Pin a paper that says 'School Drudge' on it to his coat?"

Then came Bruce's voice. "Not much," he exclaimed. "None of our old tricks this time. We'll—" but Joan was not able to catch the rest as she hurried on, across the yard, and over to her home opposite the school.

Quick tears had filled Joan's eyes. She was seeing, behind them, a merry, freckle-faced boy in overalls and jumper, a broom in his hands, as she had left him in the schoolroom just now.

"How are things going, Terrence?" she had asked as she gathered up her books and turned toward the cloak room. Terrence had smiled all over his face at her kind question.

"Fine, Joan," he had answered. "I'm sure I can hold the job until fall anyway, when the fires have to be started. Maybe they'll let me get an older boy to tend the furnace then, so mother and I can keep on. You see I do most all of the heavy cleaning here at school, and that saves mother. It's such a help to

have the basement of the school to live in.
How are the rabbits, Joan?" he asked.

"Just as darling as they can be," Joan had
said. "Thank you so much for the lettuce
you brought me for them."

Then she had left Terrence sweeping with
all the thoroughness that he had recited history that afternoon.

"It isn't fair for the boys to play tricks on
Terrence just because he is doing janitor's
work since his father died," Joan thought as
she went around to the back of the house to
look at her rabbits. Terrence had the kindest heart in the whole class, and he loved all
animals and growing things just as much as
Joan did. There was the bird house that he
had built for her in the budding apple tree,
and in a sunny corner of the yard he had
spaded a place for her flower bed. That had
been Terrence's play, though. He had so
little time for anything but work.

"What does it matter if Terrence is poor,
and if he has to get dirty, and wear old clothes?"
Joan thought. "He's just as brave and good
as he can be, and he gets better marks than
any of the other boys," she said to herself.
"He's always so kind to me; I don't want
him to feel badly." She thought a minute.
"He shan't," she decided at last as she picked

up a rabbit and held it close to her cheek. "It doesn't matter how scared I am, I'll stop it!"

The week before the first of April was so quiet in school that it seemed full of events to come. Every afternoon at the close of the session there were groups of boys to be seen in whispered consultation in the school yard. Joan saw Bruce in the hardware store down town on Saturday morning. She shivered as she ran past.

"There are all sorts of dangerous things in there," she thought, "saws, and nails, and knives! O, I do hope they're not going to do anything to hurt Terrence."

That same morning she saw Teddy coming out of the grocery store with his arms full of bundles. He did not stop to even speak to Joan, but ran by her as if he did not want her to see what he was carrying.

"Pepper and salt and all kinds of disagreeable stuff for Terrence, I'm afraid," Joan thought. "It's too bad, but I'm glad he doesn't even guess what the boys are planning."

But Terrence did know that something was in the air.

It hurt him to put on his overalls and get out his pail and mop and broom every afternoon when the other boys were playing ball or having football practice. He had not been working at the school very long, and he felt a difference in the way that the boys treated him. Lately, if he had crossed the school yard where they were talking in threes and fours, they had separated and walked off, whistling, and not noticing him. They never stayed to talk to him after the end of the class. Terrence's head bent low as he swept, and mopped, and cleaned blackboards. Not a speck of dust or a piece of waste paper escaped him, though. As he went up and down the aisles he looked at the desks to see that they were in apple-pie order.

"I must stay and try and clean off these ink spots Bruce got on his desk," Terrence said to himself the last afternoon of March. "And the boys forgot to gather up the paint cups and wash them. There's a lot of mud tracked in these days. I don't believe I shall be able to finish cleaning to-night before it gets dark, but I can do it in the morning before school begins. I'd like to go out and pitch a while, but the boys don't want me." He took a cloth and began scrubbing the untidy desk.

April dawned the next morning with the surprise of yellow sunshine and bright skies. Joan was up early and looked out of her win-

dow, and across at the school. Bruce had
asked for the key the night before, telling
her father that he and Teddy wanted to go
in early and study before school opened.
Joan could see one, two, then more boys going
stealthily in the school door and coming out
again, laughing. She could imagine what they
had been doing; she could almost see Terrence's
hurt surprise at the trap they were going to
trick him into. She ate her breakfast in
great haste, and then went over to the schoolhouse.

It seemed too lovely a day to be spoiled by
unkindness, the little girl thought. April had
planned other surprises for her children. The
first bluebird thrilled the air with a blithe
song. The grass of the schoolyard was dotted
with the first gold dandelions.

"April fools us in a nice way," Joan thought,
and just then she saw Terrence coming slowly
up from the basement, in his patched overalls,
and his shoulders bent from the heavy pail
he carried. He looked at her in surprise.

"Wait a minute, Terrence," she said. "I
want to go up to the classroom first, please."
She pushed by the boy and went up the stairs.

What would she find when she opened the
door? thought the little girl. Waiting traps
and unexpected terrors, in addition to the

things the boys had left to hurt Terrence's feeling, might be there. Joan trembled as she gripped the door knob, turned it, and then crossed the threshold.

"I won't have Terrence made an April fool; it isn't fair. I won't let them," she said over and over to herself to keep up her courage as she went bravely about the room. There was a pause. Then she opened a window and called gayly down,

"Come on up, Terrence. O, do come up just as quickly as you can."

Terrence lifted his pail and started slowly up the stairs. Somehow he felt tired that morning, and the pail and mop seemed even heavier than usual. He wished he might stay out in the brightness of the April morning a little longer, but he heard Joan's voice again.

"Hurry, Terrence, O, do hurry!"

He went slowly up to the top, set down his cleaning things, and entered the classroom. Joan, her cheeks rosy with excitement, was perched in her father's chair.

"You'd better get your broom and sweep first, Terrence," she said.

Terrence looked at her in surprise. It wasn't like Joan to treat him that way. But he went to the corner of the room where he had left the long-handled brush the night before. As he took hold of it he saw that there was a white paper tied to the handle.

"April fool!" Joan cried, as he took it off and opened it.

Terrence read in wonder what was written inside:

You thought this broom was yours, but it isn't. It belongs to you just one day a week. The rest of the week we boys are going to take turns sweeping the schoolroom so you can play. April fool!

"The whole room is full of surprises for you, Terrence," Joan said. "Go and look for them."

Filled with wonder Terrence went from one place to another. There was a second note on Bruce's desk. It read:

No more ink spots for you to clean, old man. We're going to keep our desks in order ourselves after this. April fool!

Tied to the edge of the scrap basket that he was going to empty Terrence found the new jackknife that he had looked at longingly in the hardware store, but had not been able to buy. Bruce's allowance had bought it. Inside his desk was a box of homemade taffy and nut cakes. Everyone knew that Teddy's mother made them better than anyone in town. A card on the top of the box said,

Warranted, no red pepper, or salt, or flannel.
April fool!

Terrence held his treasures in his hands and went up to Joan.

"Did you tell them to do it?" he asked.

"No, honestly I didn't," Joan laughed back at him. "I heard the boys talking about fooling you, and I was sure they were planning lots of horrid tricks just as most people do on April Fool's Day. I thought I'd come in first this morning and try to save you, Terrence. I didn't think it was a square thing for them to do. But I was an April Fool myself. The boys were only joking; I didn't understand. You see it was this they were planning all the time. You do so much for all of us, Terrence. I guess the boys want to make up by doing something for you," she finished, softly.

Terrence did not speak for a second. He couldn't, for something seemed to choke him and keep the words back; but they came at last.

"They fooled me all right," he said. "But there's one bit of it they forgot. They've made me the biggest April fool there ever was by telling me that they like me, even if I do sweep up and mop for them. I thought they didn't."

"O, we do—April Fool!" Joan said with a smile like the spring sunshine on her face.

FINDING EASTER

THE girls in Miss Janeway's class flocked out of Sunday school together, chattering like the first robins that could be heard in the orchard back of the church.

"Did you see that lovely flowered ribbon in the window of the millinery shop?" Janet Graham exclaimed. "I am going to ask mother if I can't have my Easter hat trimmed with it."

"They have ever so many new flowers too," Molly Arnold broke in, "little bunches of artificial wild flowers, and wreaths of daisies and sprays of lilacs. I want a white leghorn hat trimmed with lilacs. I think it is such a nice fashion to have a new hat for Easter. It makes one feel just like the spring, all dressed up new for Easter Day. That is what Miss Janeway spoke of to-day in class, wasn't it? She said we were to think of Easter as the time when the old things were made new."

Janet considered a minute. "Yes, I know she said that," she assented. "It seemed strange to me though, for Miss Janeway never does seem to think very much about getting new clothes for special occasions. She's go-

176

ing to wear her blue serge suit and her winter
hat for the Easter service even if she could
have silk and satin if she wanted them."
Janet puckered her forehead into a puzzled
frown as she spoke, but just then Miss Janeway appeared in the chapel door and the girls
rushed over to crowd around her.

She was not much more than a girl herself,
the daughter of the rector, and fresh from
college. She was full of the rare charm that
comes from forgetfulness of self, and her plain
clothes only served to enhance the slender
grace of her figure, the soft glints of her simply
coiled brown hair, and the lights of her deep
hazel eyes. She made blue serge take on the
regal lines of velvet through the charm of her
own winning personality. No wonder her
class in Sunday school loved her. She walked
toward the street, the girls flocking to her like
a swarm of bees flying about a flower.

"I heard what you were talking about,"
she said, laughingly. "You are all going to
blossom out Easter Sunday like a garden. Of
course you will look very pretty; but what,
for instance, is the need of Janet's covering
up her lovely hair with all that ribbon she is
thinking of having on her new hat? And Molly
doesn't need blue lilacs, for her eyes are just
that color. Do you know, girls, I have just

loved those tam-o'-shanter caps like your coats
that you have worn lately; they look so simple
and girlish. Easter comes early this year,
and you could just as well wear them a little
longer," she finished, persuasively.

Hope Dunbar looked up timidly now, a
flush of excitement lighting her pale little face.
There had been hard times at Dr. Dunbar's
since he had been called to service in the army
and left Hope and her mother with very little
to keep the home until his return. Hope
touched Miss Janeway's arm. "I think that
is such a sweet thought of yours," she said,
"but everyone does always wear something
new for Easter. You spoke about it in class
to-day. You said, 'The old things shall be
made new.'"

Miss Janeway's face lighted in the way that
the girls always said made her look like one
of the church window angels. She seemed to
be looking far off as she spoke.

"Yes, that's what Easter means," she said,
softly—"old branches living again in apple
blossoms, and buried bulbs sending up crocuses
and tulips and Easter lilies, and dead hearts
living again in faith—and the resurrection.
Don't you see, girls? We've had the wrong
idea about it for ever so long."

They had reached the gate of the rectory

now and Miss Janeway turned to the members of the class who were still about her.

"Come in, and let me make you some tea," she said. "I want to talk things over with you and see if we can't plan an Easter different from any that we have ever had here in Maywood."

Grouped around the open fire in the living room, and enjoying tea and crisp toast and strawberry jam from dainty rosebud china, the girls talked, and began to understand, and made plans.

"There's ever so much that's old in my house that I can make over, just by helping," Hope said. "I don't mean the carpets and the paint, for that would take money, but mother's old worries about how she was going to get anything new for me for Easter. I shall just tell her that I am not going to have a new hat. And there is her backache from doing all the housework since we have had to get along without a maid. I didn't think I could spare the time from my school homework to do the dishes, but I will, and iron, and dust, and make the beds too." Hope ended with an energetic nod of her curly head.

Miss Janeway put her arm around the little girl and drew her close to her. "I think that will be a most beautiful way, to make Easter blossom in a house," she said. "No new things could be better than thoughtfulness and loving helpfulness. Now, girls, I leave it all to you," she said as the early spring sunset lighted the windows, and it was time for them to go. "Tell the others and go to work every one of you, to see how much you can find in this town to make new for Easter."

It was such a different way of thinking about Easter that the girls forgot all about their clothes, except that those who were to have had new ones obtained permission to use the money their mothers would have spent to help out the wonderful plan. They held meetings at their different homes after school and on Saturday, and Maywood began to be surprised into a new kind of blooming, different from that of its orchards, and lawns, and hedges.

Hope's example was such a good one that those of the girls who found the need, and there were a good many, tried to bring about some Easter blossoming in their own homes.

"Mother hasn't had a new dress in a year," one girl confided to Hope. "She always gets something pretty for me instead, but I am just making her buy cloth for a dress, and I know I can help her make it."

Window boxes appeared to make the fronts

of bare houses more attractive. The girls raked the dead leaves from lawns, set out plants, cleaned up rubbish in the schoolyard and in the park, and a few very courageous ones painted their front fences. Janet and Molly and Miss Janeway took the leadership of the movement and tried to discover special kinds of Easter service that the girls could do. More than Miss Janeway's special class had become interested, so there was quite a group of girls to draw upon.

"The books in the Sunday school library do look so badly," Miss Janeway said one day. "The covers are torn and soiled. The new covers have come, but no one seems to have any time to take off the old ones and put on the new."

"We'll do it Monday afternoon," Hope decided, "instead of having our regular basketball practice." And they did. When the many hands had finished, the library was fresh and neat for Easter. The rows of cleanly covered books lent a distinctive brightness to the room where they were kept.

"I went by the hospital to-day," Janet said, "and so many children were looking out of the windows in the children's ward. They are the getting-better, but not-well kiddies, and, just think, they will have to stay there over Easter." She thought a moment. Then she spoke eagerly: "We girls could go and tell stories in the children's ward on visiting days, and keep it up all the spring," she exclaimed. "That would be something new and different for them."

The story hour in the hospital worked wonders. When small Peter, who had been in bed for weeks with a fractured leg, heard the story of the Little Lame Prince and realized what patience in pain can work, he began to gain.

"I don't know what's come over Peter," the nurse in the ward said to Janet one afternoon as she was leaving with her fairy books. "He's so good and so quiet."

"I know," Janet said. "He's spending his days 'way up in the clouds on a magic carpet, instead of in bed, and so he doesn't feel his splints and he's getting well faster."

It was quite true, and the same miracle thing happened to the other children. They left the ashes of their everyday suffering with Cinderella and danced with her at the ball whose joy was a veritable tonic to them. Stories of outdoors, stories of adventure, and stories of achievement helped the little convalescents to see the good, new things that awaited them when they should be well enough to leave the hospital. And the vision helped them to get well faster. The girls enjoyed the story hour as much as the children. They had never realized before how a beautiful story could make the one who heard it see life with a new vision.

Molly discovered the last work for the girls.

"Old Mr. Burns, who has the greenhouse, is so worried about his Easter trade," she told the girls about ten days before Easter. "He lost all his help when the men enlisted and he can't get anyone to help him. He says that he depends so much on the money he makes selling Easter plants to keep the greenhouse going the rest of the year."

"We'll help him," Janet announced.

So the girls put on their Camp Fire suits and went to Mr. Burns's assistance for every afternoon of the week before Easter. It seemed the happy climax to all their efforts as they worked in the rich, earth-smelling loam, and listened to the old man's homely philosophy about his growing things.

"There couldn't be anything much more discouraging looking than a rosebush shoot when you first start it," he said, "or a lily bulb. But all they need is a little encouragement, and the first you know you have roses and lilies." His words made the Easter mes-

sage come true for the girls. Every year the
earth, right there in their own town, was
holding and cherishing old things, and sending
them up new.

The girls washed flowerpots, and carefully
potted tulips, hyacinths, and daffodils under
the old florist's direction. As Easter drew near
they cut great, odorous violets and bunched
them in soft paper in boxes. They delivered
the potted and cut flowers, and passed and
repassed the milliner's window countless times
without once thinking of the artificial flowers
there, ready for Easter hats.

It had been the happiest Easter season that
they had ever known. Then it was Easter
itself, come on birds' wings through blue skies,
before they knew it. Not one was ready for
the day as they always had been before with
new frocks, and shoes, and ribbons, and gloves.
Each girl in Miss Janeway's class was prepared,
though, in a new way. Hope Dunbar put this
into words as they all met in the choir room
before they marched into church for the
Easter service.

"How nice we all look in our old things!"
she exclaimed. "I feel Easter so that it really
seems as if I am really dressed up for it."

The light shining in through the colored
windows, the sweet odor of the flowers that

banked the church, and the music that rang out with Easter joy and faith seemed more beautiful than at any Easter service before. There were so many flowers too—a bewildering profusion of color—massed at the front of the church. Old Mr. Burns, dressed in a neatly brushed black suit, sat in one of the front pews, and the girls had seen him talking to Miss Janeway before they marched in. They both looked mysterious and happy. When the service was over, the girls discovered the reason. As they filed out, the old florist took his place by the flowers and gave each girl a pot of Easter blossoms to take home.

It was part his offering, and part Miss Janeway's. As the girls went out, almost hidden by the tall lilies, bright geraniums, and purple hyacinths and heliotrope, they made a gay Easter pageant of bloom and beauty. Janet pulled her old cap down over her braids as a puff of wind met her at the door. She hugged her pot of geraniums tighter.

"Who wants an Easter hat," she laughed, "when they can have Easter this way?"

WHAT HAPPENED IN CHESTNUT GROVE

"IT seems such a little thing to do, and it will be so long growing," Janet sighed, as she put the last shovelful of earth into the hole in the schoolyard that held the new maple tree. The members of the class had bought the young tree with their own money. and were setting it out on Arbor Day. It did look discouraging, though—just a straight stick, with not a single leaf yet to show what it would do for shading the children and sheltering a nest, perhaps, in a few years.

"Mr. Burns told our class committee when they bought this tree that it would grow quicker than almost any other," Janet's friend, Bob, said encouragingly in reply. "You know he has added a nursery to his greenhouse, and he always did know just as much about trees as he does about flowers. He said that if everybody in this town would keep Arbor Day as our class is keeping it, we would have a different looking town in a few years. He said it would put Maywood on the map as far as beauty goes. He's feeling pretty badly about—" but the class was called to order just then to sing, and then came dismissal.

"What is old Mr. Burns feeling badly about?" Janet asked, remembering his words, as she and Bob started home together.

"Why, about Chestnut Grove," Bob explained. "You know it lies right next to Mr. Burns's greenhouse and his nursery, and it has been there so long that he kind of feels as if it belonged to him. He says they talked at the last town meeting of clearing it and using the land for building the new grammar school."

"O!" Janet's voice was almost tearful. "They couldn't do that, Bob, they just couldn't. Why, we've had picnics in the summer, and gone nutting in the fall, and cut Christmas greens in the winter, and looked for May flowers every spring in Chestnut Grove for years. It's the only real woods, even if it is so small, near enough for us to walk to; and it has everything that a big woods, even, could have— violets, and moss, and oaks, and evergreens, and birds. O, we can't have Chestnut Grove cleared away," she ended in a plaintive voice.

"That's just the way Mr. Burns feels about it," Bob assented, "but what can we do? We're just boys and girls, and he's only an old man, and Chestnut Grove belongs to the town," he said. "I don't see any way out of it."

"Well, let's go down and talk it over with Mr. Burns," Janet suggested. "He might have an idea."

They found the old man out in his new nursery. The rows of tree shoots and vines were growing in orderly rows, and Mr. Burns, in blue jeans and the gardener's smock that he always wore, walked up and down between the lines like a proud general, inspecting his soldiers. Beyond, like a great curtain, hiding for love all its woodsy surprises, the edges of Chestnut Grove could be seen shining in the spring sunlight. Mr. Burns was glad to see Janet and Bob. He had as warm a spot in his heart for the children as he had for his plants.

"It seems just like losing my neighbors to have those old oaks and pines cut down," Mr. Burns said when the two told him why they had come. "I can see how the town select men feel about it; the timber will bring quite a good price now and the money can go toward paying for the school. But I shall miss that nice little piece of woods."

"So shall we," Janet declared. "If there were only some way—" She was silent a moment, thinking. "O, perhaps we could—" she voiced a thought that had suddenly come to her.

It was a splendid plan. Bob added to it, and as they talked it over, Mr. Burns perfected it. Then Janet and Bob, with swift feet, went home to tell the other boys and girls about it and enlist their help.

All through the remaining days of the spring, Maywood's streets were strangely deserted of children playing. Marbles, hopscotch, jack-stones, roller skates, and push-mobiles had only an occasional interest, and there was great industry on Saturday morning in finishing errands and housework that the afternoon might be long and free. Mothers and fathers wondered a little, but the boys and girls had never had such good appetites, rosy cheeks, and bright eyes before.

"I don't know what Bob does with himself, away so much, but he doesn't seem to get into any trouble with the boys and his report card is all right." Mr. Taylor, Bob's father, said to Mrs. Taylor one night when Bob was late for supper. "We had a meeting about the new grammar school last night," he went on. I guess they'll begin cutting down Chestnut Grove in a week or so now. The school will be a good thing for the town." Bob came in just in time to catch the last words, but he did not speak as he sat down to table and made great inroads upon hot biscuit and creamed chicken. Did he and his mother exchange smiles, though, when his father was not looking? Bob's mother was one of the few Maywood mothers who had been allowed to share the secret, and she thoroughly approved.

But school was over, and Chestnut Grove put on its summer dress before anything definite was done by the town about clearing it away. The ground of the grove was covered with a soft carpet of green traced in a tra'ling pattern by the ground pine and the twin-berry vine. The trees, like columns of some great cathedral, stretched up to the roof of green leaves that they spread over the children. There were birds and squirrels and butterflies all about. It was a very beautiful bit of woods.

That was what Mr. Taylor and his committee of town selectmen thought one Saturday afternoon in the early summer when they went out to look at Chestnut Grove before letting the contract for cutting down the wood. On his way Bob's father remembered long ago days when he had gone nutting there, and cut down a Christmas tree and dragged it home. Maywood had been just a little country settlement then. Afterward, it had grown, pressing closer and nearer to the woods, but never touching the heart of them, where the cluster of chestnut trees held court among the others.

"I wonder if the children won't miss their grove," he said to himself as they reached it. Then he stopped in surprise. He took off his glasses and rubbed them and then put them on again to be sure that he had not made any mistake. No, he was not dreaming. He could read the sign nailed on a tree:

OUR TREE SCHOOL.
NO TRESPASSING.
By order of the Maywood boys and girls.

Mr. Taylor smiled, and motioned to the three other fathers to be quiet as all four peered between the bushes into the little clearing in the center of the grove. What he saw made him think of a scene from Robin Hood or A Midsummer Night's Dream.

Ever so many of the Maywood boys and girls were there, the girls wearing green cotton smocks over their dresses, and the boys brown aprons that the girls had made them. There were some rustic tables and seats made of old tree stumps and boards. At one of these tables, old Mr. Burns was going over some charts with a group of interested boys. Two other boys, with pamphlets in their hands and rules, were measuring the trunks of some of the oldest trees. A girl under Janet's direction

was nailing a rustic birds' house to a tree.
Everyone was so busy that Mr. Taylor and the
others of his committee pushed their way
softly in, and stood a moment, watching, before they were seen. Bob dropped his rule,
and a little flushed, went up to his father. Mr.
Burns stood up apologetically, and Janet put her
arms around her tree as if she wanted to save it.

"O, Dad," Bob began, "we've had this tree
school ever since Arbor Day. We cleaned up
the grove first and dug up most of the old
stumps, and cleared out the dead bushes and
brush. Then Mr. Burns sent to Washington
for the pamphlets that the government sends
free about forestry, and he has been teaching
us about tree diseases and tree surgery, and
how to estimate the amount of lumber in a
tree, and what birds that the Maywood farmers
need nest here in Chestnut Grove, and a
whole lot of other things. We thought up this
Tree School ourselves, so perhaps you'd let
us keep our woods."

"I do hope the town won't think hard of
me, sir," Mr. Burns said now, "but I've lived
next these trees so many years that they've
come to seem as close to me as friends. I
hated to think of losing them, and I always
felt that there's just about as much for young
folks to learn outdoors as inside school walls.

You see how it is. They're working harder here in vacation time than they ever did in school, and they've been at it, after school and Saturdays, all spring.'

"O, Mr. Taylor," Janet burst in now. "Please let us keep Chestnut Grove! We girls are planning to give an outdoor play here in Chestnut Grove for the Red Cross. Don't cut down the trees; we're just finding out how wonderful they are, and what they do for us, and what we can do for them."

Mr. Taylor put one hand on Bob's shoulder and reached out the other to shake Mr. Burns's hard, earth-stained one.

"You needn't worry," he assured Janet. "I guess we can speak for the town about keeping the Tree School. We just wanted our boys and girls to have the very best that there was in the way of schooling, and we can find some other site for the new grammar school. It's good for a town to have a piece of woods like this. Let's see, Jim," he turned to Mr. Burns, "didn't you and my father cut your initials in one of these old oak trees? Come and see if we can find them."

"They're having just as good a time as if they were two boys," Bob said to Janet as they followed his father and Mr. Burns in and out among the trees.

"Just listen to your father, Bob," Janet said. "He is saying that he thinks Maywood ought to have a department of forestry to watch and take care of the trees in the streets, and set out new ones when they die. He says that Mr. Burns would be the best person in the whole town to have charge of it. Isn't that splendid?"

"Arbor Day every day, isn't it?" Bob exclaimed. "Just the way it ought to be!"

WHEN MAY DAY WAS DIFFERENT

IT was because the English twins, John and
Molly Webster, were so unlike the other
boys and girls in the town that the Merrivale
children rather snubbed them.

In the first place, they looked so different
from the others. John wore a suit of thick
gray tweed with a jacket that seemed too short
and trousers that were too long. Molly wore
a dark blue flannel sailor suit, not a middy
suit, but one with an odd sailor blouse. She
had short hair and John wore his hair longer
than the boys of Merrivale did. Both John
and Molly wore woolen stockings, knitted for
them by their mother, and they wore the same
clothes to Sunday school that they did to
public school.

Because Merrivale was a little town and
nearly everyone was either related or had
been neighbors to the rest of the town, it was
hard to accept new faces and new ways. The
coming of the English twins was like a burst
of sunlight upon a whole patch of sensitive
plants. These queer little plants would shut
themselves up immediately. So did the Merrivale boys and girls in the light of John Web-

ster's honest brown eyes and the radiance of Molly's cheerful smile.

The Websters had taken the old Chapin place 'way down at the edge of the town that nobody had lived in for so long that everybody said it was haunted. They seemed to like it, although they could have afforded a better place, Merrivale said. Mr. Webster was studying soils for his government and was quite an agricultural personage at home, it was rumored. But they did the strangest things to the Chapin place.

Instead of painting the little weather-stained cottage, as everyone expected any new tenants would, the Websters left it the soft, sunny brown that the wind and rain had tinted it. Instead of putting new shingles on the roof, Mr. Webster sent all through the countryside for bundles of straw, and then he and John, with Molly and her mother helping, climbed up on ladders, and thatched the roof with the straw. At night with the windows all shining with light—the Websters never drew their curtains—passers-by said that the cottage looked alive, sitting there by the roadside. The yellow thatch was its thick hair and the glowing windows its shining eyes.

Almost every day some one had a new tale about the odd English family.

"Their mother wears a blue smock," Dorothy Adams announced at the school recess, in early April. "You know our place is next the Websters, and so I can't help seeing what is going on there. They are plowing their back lot, and Mrs. Webster went out in the field and drove the plow part of the time herself."

"And they have their supper out in the orchard now that the days are warm," Bob, Dorothy's brother, added. "They eat on a garden bench and use funny big blue bowls and plates. I bet I wouldn't want the kind of supper they have—curds and cheese and brown bread and butter and apples."

John and Molly Webster forged ahead of all the other Merrivale children in their class, though, and were always ready to help the rest. Storm or sunshine, they tramped the two miles to school and were not late once. They never thought of carrying an umbrella if it rained. They wore long capes and thick overshoes and arrived safely, their cheeks rosy and Molly's brown hair twisting into tight curls in the rain. They seemed fonder of each other than many of the Merrivale brothers and sisters. The day Dorothy Adams drew a picture of Molly in her wide, stout English boots and passed it down the aisle so that John caught a glimpse of it, he clenched his fists and his face went white with anger. He wouldn't hurt a girl though. All he did was to throw a protecting arm about Molly when school was out and hold her hand close in his as they trudged down the road toward home.

May Day fell on Saturday that year, and so the class decided to have a May party. Usually the Merrivale May parties were held in the country club with decorations of paper flowers, and supper served on the piazza to make them seem like celebration of the spring. A committee of boys and girls was appointed whose parents belonged to the country club to make the arrangements. At one of their meetings the chairman, Dorothy Adams, said:

"I don't see why we have to invite the Webster twins to the May party. They weren't in town last May Day and so they don't know anything about it. I don't suppose they have any party clothes, anyway."

And when the question of asking the twins was put to one and another after school it was decided not to.

"They probably never heard of May Day," was the common decision.

May Day dawned as if its beauty had dropped down from the sky. Golden sunshine flashed down from cloudless blue. The grass was purple with violets and the fruit trees wore fragrant white and pink cloaks. The children met at the country club for their May party early in the afternoon, but the unexpected heat of the day made the active games they had planned too strenuous. In their best clothes, they wandered up and down the piazza for an hour and wished that they were dressed for the woods and a wild flower hunt. All the town was out of doors in the Maytime except those of their May party, they thought, but they were suddenly surprised by the clear call of a bird note. There were no trees near the country club, only the rolling turf of the golf course. Where was that bird?

Again came the call, this time from the direction of the big living room of the country club. The boys and girls flocked in. Then they stood in amazement at the two quaint figures that faced them.

The fireplace had been filled with green boughs to which white tissue hawthorne blossoms had been fastened. In front of this a quaint little white gate had been built for decoration. The gate was open and inside stood a boy and girl hand in hand. The boy was dressed like a farmer of long ago—blue jeans and a wide tie and big sun hat. The girl was as winsome as if she had stepped out of one of Kate Greenaway's pictures. Her white chip hat had a wreath of pink roses. Her dimity dress had a pattern of roses, and she wore a wide pink sash tied up under her arms. Her black slippers were laced high over her white stockings and she carried a basket of pink and white paper roses on her arm.

"Who are they?" the children asked each other, but the strangers wore masks and they could not tell. All at once there came the same sweet bird call, clear and high. The farmer boy was whistling it in such a real imitation of wild birds that the robins outside began to sing too. As he stopped, the little girl by his side lifted her head and sang a quaint old song that no one there had ever heard before.

Their class teacher, who had stood unnoticed at the back, stepped out as the song ended and spoke:

"May Day is a very old holiday," she said. "It began in the time of the Druids, and everyone in the country seats of England loves to celebrate this feast of the return of the flowers. These two children have come to invite you to a real English May party."

Just then the little girl scattered her roses among the children.

"Those who have the same color may be partners," their teacher said as they all scrambled for the roses. "Follow our leaders and you will find all kinds of delightful surprises awaiting you."

Of course the secret leaked out as the merry troop of boys and girls, with the two little English country folk at their head, took their merry way from the country club and down the road toward the old Chapin place. The two unmasked and showed the rosy, laughing faces of the twins, John and Molly Webster. Surprises had begun already. No one had known that John could rival a whole forest full of birds with his whistling, and how sweetly Molly could sing! The big surprise came, though, when they all reached the twins' home.

Only their father's skill with the earth could have made a hedge of real, English hawthorne grow and bloom and English primroses dot the green grass, but there they were in all their beauty for May Day. The straw thatching of the cottage had proved a lure for the birds. It was alive with the twittering of song sparrows, swallows, and bluebirds. The house itself looked like a storybook place. All the windows were bright with flower boxes and a brass knocker and green settles on either side transformed the door. The Websters had

a real English dooryard at the back with hens
and ducks, geese, a pig and a cow, and back
of that shone their fields of newly springing
grain.

The most wonderful part of it all, though,
was the May pole. No one in Merrivale had
ever seen anything like it. It was a young
sapling tree that John had cut and stripped
clean and planted in the center of the front
yard. It was twined from root to crown with
wild vines and blossoms and hung from the
top were long pink and blue and green stream-
ers, one for each boy and girl.

Molly and John grasped, each, a streamer,
and stood on tip toe, waiting. All the others
did too, and then out came tall, dark, dignified
Mr. Webster with a fiddle to play for them
to dance around the May pole. Such gay
tunes as he was able to scrape out of it—
"Money Musk," and "Bonny Dundee," and
a host of others. The children romped
around the May pole until they were tired,
and then John and Molly led them in some
old games that were amazingly good fun.
They had three-legged races and hopping
races in the hay in the Websters' big barn.
They played battledore and shuttlecock and
tossed grace hoops on the front lawn. They
played Bean-Setting just as the country

people do in England on May Day. And
all the time John and Molly were the leaders
and best players in everything, never tiring
and always managing the game so that
everyone had a good time.

Before anyone realized it, the yellow sunlight of the happy afternoon was turned to
the soft gold that just precedes the sunset.
Suddenly the children heard a rollicking bird
call from the Webster orchard. It was John
calling them to the May Day feast which
Mrs. Webster had spread for them under the
blossom-laden apple trees. On long benches
stood delightful bowls of old English ware
brimming with thick, sweet curds. There
were thick slices of bread and butter and jam.
At each child's place was a round English
cottage cheese laid temptingly on a green leaf.
There was fruit and, to top the feast, generous
slices of pound cake. And kind Mrs. Webster
was everywhere at once with more jam or
cake.

In all their lives the Merrivale boys and
girls had never known such a happy time.
The best part of it all was that they had decided to have other good times just like it
if the Webster twins would be kind enough
to help them. For the children all saw John
and Molly with new eyes now. Just as the

lovely month of May had transformed dead
ground and bare trees into beauty, so the
sweet hospitality and unselfishness of the
little English strangers had made the other
children see their hearts.

"There's only one thing we need to make
this the best May Day we ever had," Dorothy
Adams exclaimed as they were all thinking
about going home. "We ought to have a
May Queen."

No one spoke for a moment. Everyone
was remembering the sweet singer over at the
country club, and all that she had done to
make them happy.

They all crowded about Molly as they
lifted her on to the low branch of an apple
tree and seated her there, enthroned among
the blossoms.

"Our queen!" they shouted. "Now and for
all the year!"

MAY DAY IN SCRUB ROW

"THEN it's all arranged, girls," Barbara Ashley said to the group walking home with her in the sunshine of the late April afternoon. "We will meet at my house with the lunch baskets and take the car from there to the park on May Day after school. Mother has finished a new dress for me to wear, a white flannel middy suit embroidered with blue," she added.

"I'm going to buy a two-pound box of chocolates to carry," said Janet Truesdale, Barbara's chum.

"I thought I would buy a new Camp Fire storybook, so that we could read it aloud at our May Party," another girl added.

"Splendid!" Barbara exclaimed. "We ought to have a beautiful time, and I think we'll be able to find some May flowers because it has been so warm. I'm glad, girls, that it is going to be our May Party, just for our own crowd, for we will have ever so much more fun than if we had invited outsiders. O," she ejaculated suddenly as the street narrowed and a dingy tenement loomed up at the side, "here we are at Scrub Row! Why didn't we go the other way?"

As the girls hurried along, hardly looking up at the tenements' littered fire escapes and long lines of drying clothes flapping in a kind of discouraged way in the breeze, another girl came around the corner toward them. She was just Barbara's size, but as dark as Barbara was fair, and as shabby as the latter was daintily dressed. Her big brown eyes looked in a kind of frightened doelike way from underneath long, black lashes, and as she met the girls she hugged her schoolbooks close to her to hide the patches in her much-worn coat.

"Hello, Martha," the greeting came in a rather half-hearted way from Barbara and the others.

"Hello!" Martha's reply was as full of gratitude as if the girls had given her an offering. Then she climbed the sagging stoop of the tenement and disappeared inside the dark hallway.

"Martha was at the head of our class again this month," Janet said as the girls left the shadow of Scrub Row for a wide, tree-lined street beyond.

"I don't see how she does it," Barbara continued, "going home and helping her mother wash and iron as she does. Did you notice her dress? I think she has worn it for two years now."

"You didn't ask Martha to come to our May Party, did you, Barbara?" some one queried as they reached the entrance to the modern apartment house where the Ashleys and the Truesdales lived.

"Why, no." Barbara's blue eyes opened wide with surprise. "Why should one invite Martha?" she seemed to have said. At least, that was what she implied, and it was in the thoughts of the others. Then they parted and Barbara and Janet went up in the elevator.

Barbara found her mother by the open window in the living room looking down on the mist of green that the new leaves on the trees made. She turned with a quick smile as her little daughter came in and stood by her side.

"I know just what you are thinking of, mother," Barbara said. "You are remembering spring when you were a girl in England, and wishing that you were back there now."

"O, yes," Mrs. Ashley acquiesced, "I can almost smell the hawthorne on the hedges, and hear the Maying songs that the farmers' boys and girls sang out in the fields."

"How did they keep May Day in England,

then, mother?" Barbara asked. "Did you have a party as I am going to in a park?"

"No," Mrs. Ashley said, her eyes soft with her girlhood memories. "It was the cottagers, the humble folk, who kept the May best. There was always a great tidying to get ready for it, and then they trimmed their gardens and put flowers in every window and hung boughs over the doors, and left May baskets for each other. It seemed to be the one time of the year when the poor felt rich because the earth was in blossom again. I wish there were May Days like that here in America," she finished.

"In Scrub Row," Barbara said after a moment's thought. She went into her own dainty, chintz-hung room and looked in the clothes press where the white May Day dress hung ready for the party. She touched it softly, and then went over to her dresser and opened a drawer full of fresh hair ribbons. She selected a wide blue one and slipped it in the pocket of the middy blouse. Afterward she sat down and thought.

"Among us all we'll have money enough, and Estelle's father is a florist, and May's father has a grocery store. O, I am sure that we can do it," she explained to herself. She went out into the hall and telephoned downstairs.

"Hello!—I want the Truesdales' apartment, please. O, hello! Janet, do come up right away. I have such a splendid plan in mind, and you and mother and I will talk it over together. Bring up your hat and coat, for we are going out afterward. Where are we going? O, it's kind of a secret about that. I'll tell you when you come up," she finished as she hung up the receiver.

It seemed to Martha, after she had met the girls, as if her tenement home which the town had nicknamed Scrub Row, had never seemed so shabby and forlorn before. The April sun lighted its unkempt patches of ground that could hardly be called front yards even, and showed their struggling weeds. It disclosed broken fence pickets, and missing panes of glass, and battered doors. The hallway reeked with the odor of countless washdays, and when Martha had climbed the stairs and gone into the kitchen of the little flat where she and her mother and brother Tom lived, there was a choking cloud of steam that filled the room. Her mother, bent over a tub, was doing another of her endless washings. Martha threw down her books and rolled up her sleeves.

"Sit down and rest a minute, mother," she said. "I'm home now, and I'll rub a while."

"It's spring, Martha," her mother protested.

"You ought to be outdoors breathing it," but she dropped into a chair and leaned back, weariness in every line. There was no sound for a long while except the steady rubbing of the clothes on the washboard. The soft April dusk was settling down over Scrub Row, charitably veiling it, when there was a knock at the door. Martha opened it, and then she stepped back in surprise.

"Why, Barbara—and Janet?" she exclaimed as if she were dreaming. But two merry voices laughed away her confusion, and four kind hands began urging her. "Come, Martha," the girls said, "we're making a new plan for May Day and we need you to help us. Come home and have supper at Barbara's," Janet explained. "We are going to make all the arrangements there to-night."

Strange things happened the succeeding days about Scrub Row. Tom, Martha's twelve-year-old brother, was the acknowledged leader of the Scrub Row gang. Not having any place large enough for play, the gang had always done as much mischief as it could with stones and tin cans. But the boys, headed by Tom, were busy now in other ways. They began with the Scrub Row fire escapes. Armed with a copy of the city fire ordinance they climbed up and cleared the rubbish from every fire

escape on the tenement, and a street cleaner
helped them by calling with a team to collect
and cart away the litter. It was surprising
what a difference it made in the appearance
of Scrub Row, which began at once to look
less scrubby. The boys did not stop with
the fire escapes, though. They went right to
work on Scrub Row's little front yards. They
pulled the weeds out first, and then mended
the fences, and put a coat of fresh paint on
the front doors. Barbara's crowd paid for the
paint, and it was Estelle's father, the town
florist, who arranged for Tom's gang to have
some squares for sod from the Park Department to set out in the tiny Scrub Row yards.

"Isn't it wonderful already?" Martha said
to Barbara, as the two came down the narrow
street one day after school. The girls found
Martha their right-hand helper in all their
planning now. They wondered why they had
been so blind before, seeing only her poor
clothes and shabby home, and overlooking
her fine mind and power to organize and ex-
ecute. It had been Martha who had suggested that night at Barbara's that the Scrub
Row gang be used as a clean-up squad, and
the plan had worked like magic. She clasped
her hands and her eyes shone as she looked
now at the result of their work.

"And do you know," she went on, "what the boys have done in the way of cleaning up the outside has made a difference with the flats. We always kept our curtains clean, but the family across the hall never did. Now they have put up fresh ones, and some of the other families are going to do the same. The landlord sent a man yesterday to fix all the broken panes of glass. I guess your mother asked him to do that, Barbara."

Barbara smiled. "Yes, that was one of the surprises," she assented. "But O, can you wait for the real May Day one? It seems as if I couldn't. It was so kind of the manual training teacher, wasn't it? We all had money enough to pay for the wood by going without what we had planned to buy for the May Party, and the boys have almost finished the boxes by working in the manual training room at school after hours. Estelle's father was glad to do what we asked him to."

"And May's father was too. O, it is wonderful!" Martha ended, ecstatically.

May Day was as lovely as anyone could have wished. The girls had quite forgotten their own party in the preparations for an entirely new Maying celebration that they had carried out, led by Barbara, Janet, and Martha. The night before May Day the twinkling

street lamps that shone at the entrance of
Scrub Row saw strange sights. A loaded team
drove in and stopped. There was a sound of
hammering, and exclamations of delight came
from the doors and windows of the tenement.
An odor like country fields and newly turned
earth filled the street, and then the team drove
away.

It was hard for the girls to concentrate on
lessons the first of May in school. At the
end of the afternoon session the schoolyard
fairly hummed with the girls' excitement.

"The baskets are all packed, and in the
cloak room."

"There are groceries, and fruit, and a bunch
of flowers in each one."

"Let's start now, we're all ready. Come
on, Martha, we want you to lead." The
exclamations crowded fast and merrily.

But was that really Martha who headed
the May walk, a basket on her arm, and her
soft brown hair framing a face that was bright
with rosy cheeks and shining eyes? She did
not wear the old frock and patched coat.
Instead she was dressed in a white flannel
middy suit embroidered on the sleeve and
collar with blue. A big blue bow tied her
hair, and Barbara wore her old brown serge
with a new happiness because she had given

her May Day frock to make Martha look like
the spring.

The girls started now, carrying the very
practical May baskets, and tip-toe with excitement because of what they knew they would
see in Scrub Row. But when they reached it
they could hardly believe their eyes.

"It looks like a picture place," Barbara
exclaimed.

Surely, it could no longer be called Scrub
Row, for order and neatness and beauty
reigned there. The street was tidy and the
scraps of yards were fresh and green with
their new grass. Clean curtains and polished
door knobs and fresh paint had changed the
front of the tenement, and the dull red of its
bricks took on a mellow tone in the sunlight
that was almost beautiful. But the surprise
that had transformed it was the blooming of
Scrub Row for May Day. Each flat had a
green window box filled with scarlet geraniums
and daisies. The boys of Tom's gang had
made the boxes in the school and Estelle had
prevailed upon her father, the town florist,
to fill them. The flower boxes had come and
had been set in their places on the window
sills the night before. The sun of May Day
morning had found them there, ready to bloom
and thrive all summer, and give the tenement

families a bit of brightness to lighten their work.

"Mr. Murphy says he's going to look for a better job now that he lives in such a fine Row," Martha said to Barbara as the girls went from one flat to another, leaving their baskets. "And Mrs. Bruce told mother this morning that she thinks her boy who has been ill so long feels better just for looking at the flowers in their window. I know it's going to be easier for us to do our washings with something pretty to look at," she finished, contentedly.

"Maybe there won't be any washings to do," Barbara said. "Mother has been talking to the landlord of the tenement about having one of the flats for a kind of home school where the mothers can come and learn how to cook better, and save food, and plan good meals for the children. She thinks that your mother could live in it, and help, Martha."

"O!" Martha could hardly speak. She touched the soft folds of her dress and looked at the green and the blossoms about her. "I never knew what the spring really was before," she said. "I feel it blooming in my heart; I guess that's the way it ought to come."

BORROWED MOTHERS

"YOU'LL surely come on Sunday, mother, won't you?" Edith Wainwright bent over her mother's chair and put her arms around the slender figure in black. "There's going to be a special address, and different music, and O, everybody says our Greenlawn Mother's Day will be the best one we ever had." Stopping for breath a moment, Edith placed one hand on the pile of white lawn that lay on Mrs. Wainwright's lap. "And there won't be anybody in the chorus with such a pretty dress as mine," she continued. "It was a good idea to have them all made in the same style, but mine is going to be handmade and hand-embroidered. You'll finish it in time, won't you, mother?"

Mrs. Wainwright looked up, a smile lighting her tired face. "Of course your dress will be ready, little girl. Haven't I over a week and every one of the evenings free for sewing? It has been a good deal of work, but I like to think that the dress you wear on Mother's Day will have so much of your own mother's handwork in it." She leaned back a second looking at the fine stitches she had just set, but in reality resting her eyes and flying fingers for a space.

The room looked like Edith. She had blown in like a wayward breeze, as gay and careless. A rug that she had tripped over lay in a heap, and dust from the street came in through the door that she had forgotten to close. Her books were scattered on the table and she had tipped over a scrap basket in her haste to reach her mother. Edith was a loving, thoughtless girl. Her deep blue eyes were dark now with the affection she had for this all-alone mother of hers, but her mind was busy with other thoughts.

"I'm going to basketball practice now," she said. "I promised Frances I'd stop for her. I know I ought to do the lunch dishes, mother. You haven't had time to finish them on account of the sewing, and I should get dinner, but I'm afraid I can't get home in time. You're coming on Mother's Day, aren't you, dear? Frances wants us to find out how many mothers will be there so she can tell her father."

"I'll try," her mother looked down again at her work, the tired shadows in her face covering the smile. "But the house will need a thorough cleaning the last of the week, and Lonny's croup has kept me from sleeping very much lately, and——"

"Well, you'll try to come. I'll tell Frances that." Edith pulled her hat low over her curls and darted out through the door, looking like a bluebird in her dainty blue linen and crimson tie.

Her clear call at the big white gate of the parsonage had to be repeated. Edith waited quite a time before Frances, the minister's little daughter, appeared, her white sweater over her arm and her brown eyes full of laughter.

"I thought I'd never get started," she said. "I promised father that I'd dust the library for him some day this week after school and he wanted it done to-day. I just hate to do it—taking down all those musty old books and getting my nose full of dust. I got off, though, by coaxing, and then too, father was busy and he hadn't any time to scold. He's beginning his sermon for Mother's Day. It's a nice short text, not a bit hard to remember. 'As one whom his mother comforteth, so will I comfort you.' Is your mother coming, Edith? I want to make out a list this afternoon if the girls can tell me."

"I don't know. She's been so busy since father died; we haven't any maid now, you know. Lonny has been sick and she is making me a dress, all by hand, to wear in the chorus. She said that she might be too tired to come," Edith answered, but the words and certain

of Frances's kept both little girls silent for
the rest of the way to the school gymnasium.
At the door Edith put her arm around Frances
and whispered something in her ear.

Frances laughed. Then she hugged Edith
and whispered something back to her. Both
girls giggled.

"We always do think of the same things
at just the same time, don't we, Frances?"
Edith said.

"Yes, and always the nicest things!" Frances
replied. "Now we'll have to see how the
other girls feel about it."

The basketball practice for once lagged.
Rumor flew about the gymnasium that Edith
Wainwright and Frances Giddings had a
secret; that it was a secret with a plan at-
tached and they might share it when the game
was over. So it was a few minutes before
five when a merry, laughing throng of girls, led
by Edith, put Frances on a kind of throne made
of parallel bars and a mattress, and shouted:

"Tell us about it, Frances! Please tell us!"

A flush of color rose to Frances's face, but
she tossed her loosened hair back from her
forehead and faced her mates with clear eyes.

"Maybe you'll laugh at us, girls," she began, "but Edith and I had the same idea come
to us all at once, and we'd like to see if it will

come to you too. I told Edith about the text
father is going to preach on Mother's Day—
'As one whom his mother comforteth, so will
I comfort you.' "

Frances hesitated a moment, and her voice
faltered. Then she went bravely on. "You
see I'd just run away from dusting father's
library—"

"And I'd left all the luncheon dishes without
washing them," Edith interrupted.

"So we decided to form a secret society,"
Frances went on. "It's to begin now, just as
soon as we leave the gymnasium. We're going
to have secret passwords, each one her own,
and all different. They'll be very unusual
passwords, so it will make the society unusual,
and very nice, we think. We'd love to have
anybody join who likes, only we ought to take
in as many members as we can now because
it will be confusing having so many different
passwords. Mine is 'dust cloth.' "

"And mine is 'dishpan,' " Edith added with
a decided nod of her curly head.

For a short space there was silence in the
gymnasium. A ripple of laughter at first was
immediately hushed. Then the girls began
to talk all at once.

"It's perfectly splendid, and we'll keep it
up all the year."

"Nobody will ever find out about it and we can have hikes and sewing afternoons and picnics when we get through with the regular work of the club."

"My password is going to be 'flatiron.' "

"Mine is 'broom.' "

"Mine is 'thimble.' "

The enthusiasm was contagious. Before ten minutes had passed every girl in the basketball team had joined the secret society, and they scattered at the door to begin making use of their new passwords.

Frances and Edith went up the street arm in arm, in the glow of the yellow sunset.

"They wanted to do it, really; so did we, Edith," Frances said, "only they hadn't thought of it before. Neither had we thought of it." The sound of an automobile interrupted her and the two girls saw a car coming down the tree-lined street toward them."

"There's Edward Judson," Edith said. "Doesn't he have just everything! His father lets him have his car and chauffeur almost every day after school. Hello, Edward!" She waved her hand to him.

The boy in the car motioned to the chauffeur to stop and took off his cap, a smile lighting his cheery, freckled face.

"I'm going over to the mill to get dad and

take him home," he said. "Jump in, girls, and we'll stop at the tea room and have a sundae."

"Goody. Maple walnut for me," Frances said.

"And chocolate peppermint for me!" Edith added as they drove off. It was at the little round table in the tea room, over the ice cream, that the girls told Edward about their new secret society, whispering it so that no one else could hear.

"It's fine!" Edward said as they went out: "I'd like to belong to it myself." He said good-by to the girls and started off in the direction of the mill.

Frances turned to Edith when they were alone.

"I almost told Edward that he couldn't possibly belong," she said.

"I'm glad you stopped yourself in time," Edith said. "It would have made him feel badly. Being rich doesn't make up for not having any mother."

The week before Mother's Day went by on wings. The newly formed secret society astonished its mothers by doing things at home cheerfully that had been grudged tasks before, or neglected altogether. Edith decided to wear her last year's white dress in the chorus

so that her mother might have some evenings
of rest, and she amused fretty little Lonny,
and made good use of her password.   Dr.
Giddings found his library as neatly dusted
as if elves had been at work in it.   The other
girls got up early without being called, and
played seamstress, and waitress, and kitchen
maid, and gardener at home, with the result
that the mothers of Greenlawn could hardly
understand the change in their daughters.
But it was a comfort to be able to rest weary
feet and hands and get ready for Mother's Day.

The day was a most lovely one.   The girls
were bubbling over with happiness, for their
work had been made merry by its secrecy.
It had been such fun to give the passwords
in school and mystify the boys, who could
not seem to understand their significance.   The
boys and girls in Greenlawn Grammar School
were particularly good friends.   The girls were
apt to attend the baseball matches in a body
and bring sandwiches and ice-cold lemonade of
their own making.   The boys, in return, were
always ready to put up swings for a picnic
or shift scenes for a school play.

"I believe the boys are a little bit hurt
because we haven't let them come in our
society," Frances said to her father as they
walked beneath the leafy bower of the trees

toward the little gray stone church on Mother's
Day. "But what could they have done in it?
We've never done anything before without
Edward, but he hasn't any mother."

The minister put his hand on his beloved
little daughter's shoulder.

"So many in the world have no mothers," he
said, "but that is one reason why we have this
day. We want to share our mothering; mother
love, and mother care, and mother spirit."
Then he suddenly stopped, putting on his
eyeglasses as he looked up the street.

"What is that?" he asked. "Look, Frances;
it seems to be a kind of procession."

It was a procession of boys, but they were
not alone. Heading it was an automobile full
of old ladies. They had each a bright nosegay pinned to their shabby black frocks and
they were rivaling the day in the sunshine of
their smiles. Following were more old ladies
carefully escorted by boys. All had bouquets,
and the boys wore their best suits and their
very best manners.

"It's our boys!" Frances exclaimed.
"They're stopping at the church."

The two hastened and reached the churchyard just as Edward got out of the car and
opened the door to let out his party of delighted guests. The other boys ushered their

charges in the gate, pretending not to notice the girls, but addressing strange words to each other.

"Wood basket!"

"Grocery list!"

"Clothes line!"

Edward was the most mystifying of all. He said "Green tea," in an undertone to Edith as he helped a particularly old lady of his automobile party up the church steps. Moreover, the mothers of the boys, who had come earlier, seemed to be in the secret too, for they could be seen nodding and laughing to one another. Each one wore a beautiful bouquet of flowers and a particularly happy expression.

Frances looked up laughingly into her father's face.

"Passwords!" she said. "The boys got even with us. You see, our secret society is to have a Mother's Day at home every day, but we didn't tell the boys about it, only just Edward. They always say they can do things just as well as we can. Edward must have told them, and they've not only done all that we have done, but they've brought all the old ladies from the Poor Farm."

The minister stood beside the gate, his hat off as the last of the boys' borrowed mothers went inside. Their eyes were dim from a great many years of watching, their fingers were twisted and bent from the toil that had gone without its reward, leaving only the scars. But they had shining faces, and not one was without a nosegay or a boy to escort her to church.

The music of the prelude poured out of the door, and in a tree in the churchyard a mother bird sang above her nest.

"Wasn't it nice of the boys?" Frances said as she joined Edith.

"As one whom his mother comforteth!" her father said, going inside. "Every one of them comforted!"

TAD'S DECORATION DAY

EVERYBODY in Hill Top knew Tad
Brewster, the florist's boy. Everybody
loved Tad too, for, although his lameness
kept him home from school a good deal, and
he had long nights of sharp, hard pain, he
was just about the cheeriest boy in all the
village.

The Hill Top boys and girls were always
glad of an excuse to do an errand to the big
corner place with its wide cultivated fields
and low-roofed buildings that made the greenhouse. A new flowerpot to replace a broken
one, a cartful of rich earth, a bunch of cuttings
—these were all seized upon as opportunities
for spending a little while with the merry,
freckle-faced boy whose crutches did not keep
him from getting about with his visitors, and
whose happy laughter could equal theirs.

Living with the plants and helping his
father as much as he did gave Tad a kind of
canny cleverness with growing things. He
could straighten a bent vine and make it twine
and flourish again. He was able to coax a
blossom from the most stubborn root or seed,
and when there was nothing else for him to

do, Tad would sit for hours in the sunny door of the green house twisting and weaving twigs and wires to make baskets for his loved plants.

Decoration Day in Hill Top was always one of the most celebrated holidays of the whole year. In all the seasons that had passed since its Old Guard had returned home, carrying the battered Stars and Stripes and gloriously proud of its record in spite of its depleted numbers, Hill Top had never forgotten to honor its veterans. There was only a handful of the soldiers left now, but they marched with the old flag every Decoration Day, followed by the Hill Top school boys and girls carrying their plants to God's Acre on the hillside.

The best part of Decoration Day in Hill Top was that the children bought their own plants. They saved or earned for a long time beforehand for the bright red and pink geraniums, the heliotrope and ivy plants that they carried in the parade. Tad was in his glory for weeks before Decoration Day because the children came, before school and after school, to ask his advice about how best they could spend their Decoration Day money. He would hobble out to the gate to meet them, his eyes shining with excitement as he gave them the latest news of the spring.

"I'd buy a Martha Washington geranium if

I were you, Bob," he would say. "They're finer than ever this season and thick with buds. Or, if you like, there is the Snow on the Mountain. That's a long bloomer, and if you like a pink geranium there's nothing finer. I know all the geraniums are going to be fine this year though. I helped set out the slips, and they were good healthy ones."

"Tad will tell you what you can get the most of for Decoration Day for fifteen cents," one boy or girl said to another in the school recess. "Wish he could march with us," they added. Back of the happiness and excitement of carrying their bright flowers and tramping along in time to "The Battle Hymn of the Republic" with the old veterans, was the longing in the heart of each boy and girl to have Tad there too. He was with them, in a way; his earth-stained fingers and patient toil at the roots of each plant they carried. But to have Tad able to walk briskly along with the band, how they would have loved that! Tad never told how deeply this was his wish too. He only stood at the gate, waving to them as they passed on Decoration Day morning.

Janet Makepiece, who was Tad's nearest neighbor, learned of his Decoration Day plan and she couldn't keep the secret. It spilled over one day after school.

"Tad's going to celebrate Decoration Day himself this year," she said. "He told me about it yesterday when I went over to order my plant. He's got one corner of the greenhouse full of the nicest, special kinds of plants that he has raised all himself—a lily in blossom, and a pink rambler rose, and some baskets of ivy and geraniums that will grow all summer because they're in earth."

"But Tad can't march in the parade."

"What is he going to do with those plants?"

"He never has celebrated Decoration Day."

The children's comments came thick and fast.

"Well," Janet's brown eyes grew very tender and her bright face was a little sober as she spoke, "Tad says that his father was talking to him the other night about what they do over in England to people who are brave like our soldiers. You know Tad's father used to be the head gardener on an estate in England. He told Tad that they don't wait until people die to decorate them. They put Victoria crosses and decorations like that on brave people while they are alive. Of course we do give people medals here, but we don't celebrate a special day for it. Tad said he got to thinking of all the people in this town who deserve to be decorated and whom nobody even thinks

of on Decoration Day. There's Mrs. Murphy
who's done washing in Hill Top for thirty
years and carried it home, rain or shine, and
has chilblains so she can hardly hang things
out now. Tad's going to send over one of his
flower baskets to hang in her kitchen window.
He spoke of Mr. Jerry Brown, the pound
master, too. You know he is obliged to catch
all the stray dogs in the town and put them
in his pound, but he feeds them himself, and
he gives them a better time than they ever
had before. Tad's going to give Mr. Jerry
something too."

The children were as excited as Janet when
she finished telling them about Tad's decorations.

"We might do it, too," Janet suggested.
"We've all saved up our money for Decoration
Day, and what we don't spend for flowers
we could use to do what Tad is doing—decorate
live people who deserve it. And why can't
we help Tad deliver his plants? He never can
get around with them all?" she suggested.

"Goody!"

"Janet and Tad always do have the best
ideas!"

"We can meet at my house and make plans."

"We've got ten days before Decoration Day."

The breathless sentences whirled their way

through the group; but one was whispered. The suggestion it carried was a secret. It was such a jolly secret that the children clapped their hands and shouted at the joy of it.

Tad did not seem to mind the fact that his secret had leaked out. He hobbled gleefully with any boys and girls who came to see him over to his own special corner of the greenhouse and showed them his precious store of plant decorations.

"If I could buy the brave people medals or something like that, I'd like it better," he said, "but these are my very best plants and they'll last a good while with care."

Putting their heads together with Tad, the children made plans for using what little they could scrape together in making their Decoration Day offerings to the brave people of Hill Top. They planned how they could do something for each one of the old veterans who were left. Corporal Baxter needed a new tip to his wooden leg, and they found out how much it would cost and wrapped up the money for it in a little silk flag. Colonel Brown wanted a new pipe, and Janet's father carved him a brierwood one. The gold cord and tassel on old Private Munson's Grand Army hat was ragged and tarnished, but Bud Jennings's father, who had the Hill Top dry goods store, sent to

Boston and bought a new cord, as shining as gold, with Bud's money. Altogether, the children thought that they had never had such a fine time in all their lives as during those crowded ten days before Decoration Day.

Strange to say, though, Tad was not happy.

He couldn't exactly put his trouble into words, and if the boys and girls of Hill Top had realized that they were the cause of it they would have been heartbroken. Tad felt suddenly that he wasn't really one of them. He had never felt this before, and they were most unintentional slights that hurt him now.

"I can't stay any longer, Tad," Janet said. "We're having a meeting in Bud's barn. No, I can't tell you what it's about; it's a secret."

Two or three children come to buy plants would begin whispering together when Tad's back was turned and then motion for silence when he turned back. Tad wouldn't have cried for the world; he never had even in the long nights of his pain when it seemed as if he couldn't bear it any longer. As he watched the children scatter in close groups, all conversing eagerly, or saw them running home on their good legs, he would sit down in the greenhouse door and think it all over.

"I can't really belong to them," he said to himself. "They try to make me feel that I do, but they will always be able to do things better and get to places quicker than I can. I'm a cripple—nothing else."

Decoration Day dawned so beautifully in Hill Top that it did not need the yards of flying bunting that draped the houses to greet it. The sky was cloudless blue. The hillsides were star-sown with white daisies, and early roses in the gardens gave their crimson to complete the colors of the day. The children were up with the sun delivering Tad's flowers and their own offerings. They had made special tags with the American flag painted on each.

"A Decoration Day remembrance for a brave person who deserves to be decorated," the tags read.

Everyone said that it was the best celebration Hill Top had ever had, and by nine o'clock the parade began to muster in the town square.

The veterans led off as briskly as they could, and the band came next, hardly stopping for breath between tunes. Following the band came the Hill Top boys and girls. The boys wore their blue serge suits with white blouses and small flags in their buttonholes. The girls were in white with red or blue hair ribbons. Each carried a plant, the red of the geranium blossom and the bluish tint of the heliotrope adding to the color scheme. As the parade, including the town guard and a committee of citizens, swung out of the square and toward the end of the town, it made a very gallant showing indeed.

The greenhouse and its grounds were stripped of bloom. Tad, dressed in his best suit, hobbled about looking at the frames and empty holes in the ground where his plants had been. Then he went out to the gate to watch for the Decoration Day parade. It had to pass his place. He listened. Yes, there was the crash of the brass instruments coming nearer all the time. There was a rising cloud of yellow dust. Tad's eyes flashed and he pulled himself up as straight as he could on his crutches. Then he remembered his new hurt. He had done all he could for Decoration Day, but he couldn't really be a part of it. His life was as empty as the greenhouse, stripped of its flowers. Tad shrank back as the brave company came into sight, gay with music and bright with its country's colors.

"It'll be by in a minute now," he thought. "They won't see me and I don't believe I want to see the parade as much as I did last year."

But the cloud of dust grew thicker and then it settled, leaving the road golden with its paving of sunshine. The band was still. The parade had stopped directly in front of the greenhouse and Tad heard the voices of his boy and girl friends shouting:

"Tad! Tad! Three cheers for Tad. Come out and get your decoration."

Tad swung out through the gate on his crutch and faced the line of veterans and children. It dazed him to see the white, the red and blue of the parade, but Janet stepped out of the line and went up to him. Her voice brought him back to the realization of the scene.

"This is for you, Tad," she said. "We children got it for you because we think that you deserve to be decorated more than anybody else in Hill Top."

As she finished speaking, Janet took a great, beautiful flag from the veteran who was carrying it and folded it about Tad's crooked shoulders.

"We kept it for a secret," she said. "You never guessed, did you, Tad?"

It wasn't a dream. The old soldiers had taken off their hats to him and the band had struck up "Hail to the Chief."

Tad watched the parade march on until it was only a speck of color in the distance, hugging the flag to his heart. What did it matter that he couldn't go with them? There wasn't a happier boy in the world than he with his precious decoration of Old Glory.

EARNING THE FLAG

"IT'S silk!" came in interested whispers from the corner of the assembly room where Five A sat.

"There isn't another flag like it in the Chestnut Street School," Five B declared. "Look at the cord and tassel and the gilt eagle on top."

"The Chestnut Street kids will get it, of course; Chestnut Street first, and no chance for Long Pond," was the almost sullen murmur from the back of the room where the factory district boys and girls sat, not really belonging in the beautiful new brick school but transferred there for the term on account of crowded conditions in their own district.

But all the excited comments from the Grades were hushed as the principal of the school, Dr. Newton, rose and standing by the beautiful Stars and Stripes on the platform explained it.

"Flag Day is always a different day from any other patriotic holiday," he said. "It was celebrated first in our country to give us an extra chance to honor Old Glory. Particularly ought we to honor it in a fine way this year through some kind of service for our country. So the school system of our town of Waterford that has grown so much since our factories went up and our new neighbors, the workmen in them, are with us, has bought this flag for the boys and girls. It is to be given to the class that shows the finest, largest kind of patriotism between now and Flag Day, June fourteenth. You have almost a month; make it count. You are to choose and carry out your own kind of patriotism. The morning of Flag Day, we will meet here again, and talk it all over and see who has earned the Stars and Stripes. Three cheers, now, for Old Glory!"

The hall echoed with them. Later, in the classroom, it was hard to settle down to problems in percentage and dates in ancient history. Wasn't history of to-day in the making right there before them in the silk folds of the flag, that each class felt sure it was going to earn? There was good reason too for their hopes. They talked them over in the yard that noon.

"Thirty service flags; there's a flag with one star at least in it in the window of each of our houses," Jack Burden, the acknowledged leader of Five A, boasted proudly. "Some of our fathers or brothers, or sisters are serving their country. If that doesn't make the patriotism of Five B I don't know what could. I guess the flag's ours right now, without any more bother."

It did seem as if it really were; no one spoke for a moment, and then Marjory Blake touched Jack's sleeve gently. "I know that's a splendid showing, Jack," she said, "but our Junior Red Cross in Five B has a larger membership, and has done more knitting than any other Junior Chapter in the county. It seems as if that ought to count. Don't you think that it may, Jack?"

Jack looked down kindly into the flushed, upturned face of his girl friend and neighbor, Marjory. He wanted to encourage her, but he was anxious to see the new flag floating in his own classroom on Flag Day.

"Maybe so; Dr. Newton will decide, and—" Then he was interrupted. A flying figure, fists clinched, his cap worn awry, and his dark, tanned face still darker with anger, broke into the group of Chestnut Street boys and girls.

"They say over there in the corner of the yard that we can't even try for the American flag," the boy burst out. "They say we're not Americans, but I say we work for you. My father is an iron molder. He can bend iron to make an engine or the bow of a ship. He can stand the heat from a furnace door and not be afraid. He will work all night. I say we are Americans down at Long Pond!" The boy stopped, out of breath.

Jack put his hand on the lad's shoulder. He couldn't help liking this Russian boy, Boris, quick to fight, and as quick to shake hands again; with the folk stories of his home country at his tongue's end, and wits for his studies that all his mates envied. Still, he was in the wrong now.

"Cut it out, Boris," Jack advised, good-naturedly. "We know just how you feel about it, and of course, you and Angelo and Dutchy and all the others from Long Pond will be Americans when you grow up and take out your papers, but you're not citizens yet. Don't feel badly about it, old man, but if I were in your place I wouldn't bother much about working for the flag. If it were one of your own flags, or Angelo's now, it would be different, but—well, you see how it is—*we're* the Americans," he ended, conclusively.

Boris's face paled a little, and his hands dropped at his sides. Jack was his hero, in class work, games, everything; he believed in him implicitly. Then he turned to the little girl who was his friend also.

Marjory smiled kindly, but she shook her brown curls emphatically to show that she agreed with Jack.

"I think Jack's right, Boris," she said. "I'm awfully sorry, and if it were only you I wouldn't mind. But"—she glanced across the schoolyard at the motley crew of foreign boys and girls in old boots and bright shawls, now occupied in eating their various luncheons from the depths of red bandanna handkerchiefs—"you must see how it is, Boris: it's just got to be our flag. I don't know what you could do to get it."

Boris was silent. He couldn't understand, but he took his friends' word for it. He loved the Stars and Stripes. They had guided his steps down the gangplank of the great ship that had brought him and his mother and father to this wonderful land of the free. The flag flew over the schoolhouse where he was learning the things that only the rich boys in his own country were privileged to learn. And there was the little cottage down at Long Pond, with its pocket-size garden, and a boat on the water, and no landholder to come and collect tithes. It was under the shadow of the great factory whose shrill whistle was a kind of trumpet call to Boris every day. The factory's huge masses of black smoke twisting up to the blue sky seemed to the boy like the genii of a fairy tale, pointing the track that great aircraft would take, propelled by the engines his father helped to make. But he wasn't an American, and he couldn't try to earn the flag for his class. Boris turned quickly and dropped his head. He didn't want Jack to see the tears that had welled themselves into his eyes.

Those were busy days that followed. Jack and the others in his class made out a careful record of the absent ones in service for the colors from each of the Five A homes. It was a splendid showing, Army, Navy, Red Cross, medical, one chaplain, and many Y. M. C. A. workers. Marjory's class Chapter of the Junior Red Cross had a fair that netted quite a sum for the treasury, and then arranged some tableaux to give the afternoon before Flag Day. Other classes wrote compositions on town history, made current event scrapbooks, and learned patriotic recitations to give in honor of the Stars and Stripes. The long blue days of May and the beginning of June were happily full of these preparations. Trees burst into green, lawns were dotted with tulips and daffodils, and rosebushes budded. The earth seemed very good indeed, and peaceful, in spite of daily war news. Then the unexpected happened. The Long Pond factory men went out on strike.

No one had realized, until Waterford's quiet, tree-lined Main Street overflowed with the Pond's foreign element, how large a settlement had sprung up, in the mushroomlike cottages about the aircraft factory. The dark, soot-begrimed workmen, sullen and defiant, walked the streets all day, and gathered in threatening groups at the corners at night.

"They don't seem to know what they want," Jack said to Marjory on the morning of Flag Day. He had stopped at the little girl's house to take her to school, for her mother thought the streets were too unsafe for her alone. "Father said they had a meeting in the town hall last night, and an engineer from the government was there, telling them all about what wonderful things American aeroplanes are going to do for our country, and how the men are keeping it all back by stopping work. Boris's father is a kind of leader of the factory men, and Boris was there with his mother. But the men wouldn't listen to the engineer; they just hissed him and walked out."

"Well, one trouble, I think, is that they don't understand English well enough," Marjory said, wisely. "Now, if they were only all like Boris—"

"O, Boris!" Jack commented, as if the lad's name alone spelled understanding. "Here we are," he went on as they turned in at the school door, "and we'll find out if it's your class, or mine that gets Old Glory!"

There was a hush of the unusual over the Flag Day Assembly, though. Everyone felt that the town's patriotism had been hurt by the walkout at the factory. "America" and "The Star-Spangled Banner" seemed, somehow, to be sung less heartily, and there were big gaps in the Long Pond places. Many of the boys and girls were absent, or straggled in late and looking sullen. Boris was noticeably absent.

The opening exercises were about over when there was a stir at the back of the room. The door opened, and a dark-browed giant of a man came in and walked down the aisle to the platform. He was followed by Boris, flushed with embarrassment.

"Boris's father," Jack whispered to a friend. "He looks like the giant smith, Vulcan, doesn't he?"

The Russian spoke in broken English to Dr. Newton, who looked first surprised, and then amazed. As the man started to go, Dr. Newton detained him and Boris also. He spoke to the assembly.

"Boris's father came to explain why he is tardy," he said. "It is for such an unusual reason that I want Boris himself to tell his mates of our Chestnut Street School. Tell them, lad; don't be afraid," Dr. Newton said.

Boris hesitated, drew a quick breath, and then began speaking, his clear voice reaching to the very end of the room.

"It was about the strike at the factory," Boris said. "My mother and I went to a meeting about it, and I listened to what an American said about needing my father's work at the factory. 'A great factory,' he said, 'and a great American citizen would work in it for his country without striking, and the czar of this country would see that he was treated fair.' So I talked it over with my father afterward, and told him that this was how he could be an American, and I too. I told Angelo to tell his father, and Dutchy his. We went to all the Long Pond boys this morning, and they asked their fathers to be Americans and go back to work in the factory. My father goes now to his work with the others," Boris finished, simply.

As the children looked at Boris and his father, the latter standing there with his sleeves rolled up so that the great knotted sinews in his arms showed, it seemed to them that a great moving picture were unfolding itself before them. Under the Stars and Stripes marched the soldiers who defended it, and the sailors, but following them came the laborers, strangers in our land, but molders of metal and pounders of rock, giving the nation transportation and roads, and tilling the soil to provide food for the country. It seemed the most natural thing in the world for Dr. Newton to put the prize flag into Boris's arms, where its folds touched his father too. The room was one great voice with the cheers of the boys and girls, and when they grew quiet, Dr. Newton spoke again.

"I wish that we had a flag for each class that has done so much to deserve it," he said, "but Boris has done something for his country without any thought of reward, and it is a very great achievement."

"Hurrah for Boris!" they had begun again.

"Boris—American!" Jack's voice could be heard shrilly above the others.

IN THE TRAIL OF A BULLET

"WHY can't I have just a small pistol for Fourth of July? I'm only going to shoot at a mark; I won't do any harm with it, father?" Judson Alwyn begged. "I'll buy it with my own money and you know I promised to go without fireworks this year. They've got some for only a small bullet down at the hardware store. Can't I get one of those, father?"

Mr. Alwyn glanced up from the desk in his study, a sober look on his face.

"There was an account in this morning's paper of a very small and innocent-seeming pistol in a boy's hands that killed his little sister," he said. "I don't expect any such carelessness from you, Judson, but I wanted you to set an example this Independence Day for the other boys in your class. Going without fireworks and spending the money for a pistol is hardly doing that, son."

"But, father," Judson persisted, "if I just shoot it off in our yard?"

Mr. Alwyn thought a moment. Then he reached out his hand and laid it on the boy's shoulder.

"I shall let you use your own judgment about getting a pistol," he said. "You will be thirteen years old the first of July, and perhaps you would like to celebrate the Fourth with your own independence. I can't always decide matters of this kind for you. Your best way of learning is to decide them for yourself. But don't forget, son, what may follow in the trail of a bullet."

Judson's eyes shone.

"You're awfully good, dad!" he said. "I'll be careful. You won't be sorry that you trusted me." He was off like a whirlwind to his own room to count his allowance.

But during the days that passed before the Fourth Judson's conscience worked overtime. His father's gift to him on his birthday was a two-and-a-half dollar gold piece. Judson held it in the palm of his hand and watched the sunlight flash on its glittering surface. Now he could buy a pistol without feeling any loss of pocket money, but he found it hard to look straight in his father's eyes as he thanked him for the gift. Perhaps he would not buy the pistol after all, he thought.

But the day before Fourth of July all Judson's qualms of conscience left him. The occasional snapping of caps or the explosion of a cannon cracker by some forehanded boy was like touching fire to Judson's sleeping desire.   He stuffed a bill in his pocket, went down to the store and came home with the pistol he wanted, so small and apparently harmless that he wondered at his father's warning.

Independence Day began with blazing sunshine that made the town's flags gloriously bright. Judson was out early, going down to the park to look at the band stand.   Then the sun clouded and a July rain began to drip down.   Judson turned up his collar and pulled down his cap as he ran home.

"I'm glad I didn't spend any money on rockets or pin wheels," he said to himself. "It's going to be wet all day. and there won't be much chance to send off fireworks to-night. I'll shoot a little in the back yard, though, before it pours any harder.   That's what I told father I was going to do—just shoot at a mark."

Judson had reached home now and went around to the back of the house.   He looked about for a target.   The storm had blown down a small branch from an apple tree with a tiny green apple on it, and the branch hung where the wind had carried it on a telephone wire.

"I'll play I'm William Tell shooting at the apple on his little boy's head," Judson thought.

He took aim, fired, but missed the apple. A second time also he missed it. The third shot was successful. It split the apple through the center. Judson smiled with satisfaction and went into the shed out of the rain. He had decided to keep his pistol in his tool chest there.

Judson had spent an hour in the shed, working at his bench on a toy boat he was building, when he heard a quick call from the house.

"Judson! Come, Judson!" It was his father's voice, and was sharp with excitement.

Judson ran in through the kitchen and into the living room. His mother lay on the couch while his father was trying to stop the flow of blood from a jagged cut in her wrist with an arm tourniquet.

"The glass fell out of the door in the kitchen cabinet," Judson's father explained, "and it cut your mother's wrist badly. I can't leave her. Telephone for the doctor, Judson."

Judson was almost as pale as his mother as he darted into the hall and took down the receiver. He put it to his ear and waited for a period that seemed hours. It was only seconds, but there was no answer from central to his call. Judson moved the receiver hook up and down impatiently. There were moments of waiting now, but still came no response from the central office.

"They don't answer! What shall I do, father?" Judson asked.

"Run as fast as you can to the doctor's office," his father said. "Perhaps the telephone's out of order."

Judson put on his cap and sprinted uptown. The doctor's office was half a mile away, but he covered the distance in record time. His quick ring at the door brought the doctor's wife.

"What is it, Judson?" she asked as she looked at the boy's flushed face.

"Mother's hurt and we need the doctor right away," Judson panted.

The doctor's wife looked worried. "I don't know what to do," she said. "Malcolm Brainard burned himself with his toy cannon and the doctor was called there just now to dress his burns. He couldn't possibly be through yet, but I'll call up the Brainards. Come in, Judson, and sit down while I telephone."

The telephone connection was near the front door in the hall. Judson went in, but he was too frightened to do anything but watch as the doctor's wife put the receiver to her ear, and listened, and waited.

"It's very strange," she said at last. "Central doesn't answer at all."

"That's what happened over at our house," Judson said. "I couldn't get you, so I came over."

"Well, you run down to the Brainards' yourself, Judson," the doctor's wife said. "Tell the doctor about your mother and see what he says."

The blocks to the Brainards' house seemed like miles to Judson. In the house he saw his friend, Malcolm, wrapped in bandages, and the good doctor bent over him, hardly looking up from his work of easing the boy's pain as he answered Judson.

"I can't leave Malcolm alone. If you could get Miss Janeway, the nurse, to come and finish these dressings, I could go to your mother. Her telephone is ninety-one. Try the telephone office, Judson. The telephone here seems to be out of order. I just tried to get the drug store and couldn't even get central."

The telephone office was around the corner from the Brainards'. As Judson pulled a nickel out of his pocket and went in the door he saw the emergency wagon and force outside.

"Sorry; you can't telephone, my boy," the girl in charge of the booths said to Judson. "Every telephone in this town is dead—one thousand. Such a situation never came about before. We've got to send the force out to see what's the matter."

"O, there's Miss Janeway now!" Judson exclaimed, as he caught sight of a trim little woman in a nurse's uniform and carrying a bag passing the telephone office.

"O, Miss Janeway," he gasped, running out to her, "the doctor wants to know if you will come up to the Brainards' and finish dressing Malcolm's burns, so he can go to our house. Mother's hurt."

The nurse's response was an instant "Yes," and a few minutes after she had entered the Brainards' home. Judson saw the doctor come out of the house and start his car speeding in the direction of their home.

The rain was over and the sun was again shining. Judson felt as if the storm of anxiety through which he had gone the last half hour had also cleared.

"Mother will be all right now," he thought. "Funny, though, it is about all the telephones in town being out of order. It looks as if they were keeping Independence Day. It must make a lot of trouble, for there isn't any way of getting the fire department, or the police station, or the gas office, or the telegraph office by telephone. My, but I'm tired! I think I'll walk home instead of running," he decided.

As Judson started home he seemed to meet at every step new difficulties caused by the dead telephone system. Telephone company employees who should have been enjoying the Fourth as a holiday were busy climbing high poles and testing wires. He met his friend, Bob Jennings, running like the wind. To his, "Wait a minute, Bob! What's your hurry?" Bob called back:

"Can't; dad's got to go out of town in a hurry on business and we couldn't 'phone the station to find out about the holiday schedule of trains. I've got to go two miles to get him a time-table."

At the park a disappointed crowd waited around the bandstand.

"The band master's ill, and there isn't any way of telephoning over to the next town for another conductor," Judson heard a boy in the crowd explain.

When he finally reached home Judson found his mother sitting up in an arm chair, her wrist properly bandaged, and her face pink once more.

"Father and I will get supper, mother," Judson said. "It will be a fine way of celebrating. We'll do some scout cooking. Is there any bacon in the house?"

"Not a bit," his mother laughed.

"And no telephone to order any," Judson's father said.

"Well, we'll make biscuits and an omelet," Judson decided. "It would be jolly if we could have ice cream for Fourth of July, wouldn't it?"

"We could," his mother said, "but we would have to telephone for it."

"O, look!" Judson exclaimed just then. "The telephone men have come as far as our house. They're out in the back yard now. One of them is 'way up the pole, mother, working at a cable. Did I tell you that not a single telephone in this town has been working for several hours?"

Judson went out to the kitchen and opened the door into the yard, watching the man on the pole. He was boring inside the cable. Suddenly he appeared to take something out which he held up and looked at in surprise. He came down the pole, and to Judson's astonishment crossed the yard and came as far as the door.

"Where's your father, boy?" the telephone man asked.

"He's here. Come in," Judson said.

He followed the man into his father's study and listened as he spoke.

"I'm sorry to disturb you, Mr. Alwyn," he said, "but I thought you'd be interested to see what we've found." He opened his hand and laid a small twenty-two caliber bullet on Mr. Alwyn's desk.

"It was inside the lead casing of the telephone cable," he said. "It made a hole in it that let the rain in and short-circuited every telephone in town. I don't know how it got there, and it's just luck that I found it. We might have looked hours longer for the trouble and not located it. I thought you might like to keep the bullet as a souvenir, sir."

After the telephone man had gone, Judson's father held the bullet in his hand, looking from the bit of lead to Judson and then back to the bullet. Judson could not speak. At last he went out to the shed and returned with his pistol which he put in his father's hands.

"I didn't know it could make so much trouble," he said, manfully. "I was only shooting at a mark, but the bullet did have a long trail, father."

"It couldn't have had a much longer one. You hit the whole town, son," his father said as he laid the pistol in the top drawer of his desk.

GLADYS'S RED, WHITE, AND BLUE DAY

"THE roses are opening, mother," Gladys exclaimed as she wheeled herself in her invalid's chair down the gravel walk and as far as the white garden gate over which the red rambler climbed. "I can reach them when I stretch my arms up, even if I can't stand."

Gladys's mother looked up from the pan of green peas she was shelling on the piazza and smiled, even though it was rather like sunshine glinting through a mist of tears.

"I'll bring out the garden shears, Glad," she said, "and you may cut as many roses as you can reach and make them into nosegays to give to the girls when they go by to school."

"O, may I?" The little girl's eyes were shining with joy as she took the big shears from her mother's hand and pulled herself up as far as her helpless limbs would let her. Snip, snip, the sweet blossoms dropped down into the lap of her pink gingham dress.

"No, don't help me, mother," she insisted. "When I reach up like this I feel almost as if I could walk. I shall walk in a few months now, you know—the doctor said I would. It isn't as if I were going to be paralyzed always. I'm getting better every day," she ended, happily.

Her mother dropped a kiss on the little girl's upturned face and laid her hand tenderly on her soft hair. In spite of the illness that had left her so helpless a year before, Gladys looked like the summer epitomized in girlhood. Her eyes reflected the sky's own blue, and her hair caught and held the sunshine as the breezes tossed it about her rosy face.

She wheeled closer to the gate now, leaning forward and looking eagerly up the street.

"It's a quarter after eight. The girls will be coming past on their way to school soon," her mother said. "I'll finish shelling the peas, Glad, so I can come out and work in the garden near you after they've gone."

"All right. O, there's Betty Porter now!" Gladys exclaimed as she held a bunch of the rambler roses high over her head and waved them gaily toward the girl who came flying down the street, her school bag swinging over her shoulder.

"I'm early, Glad," Betty said as she stopped at the gate and perched on the arm of the little invalid's chair. "But then we girls haven't been late for school once, Glad, since you've had to stay home and have waited here for

us every morning. Miss Jennings says you've
raised the standard of our class in attendance
just by having to be away from school yourself, Glad!"

"O, did she say that?" Gladys's face shone
with happiness. Then she reached toward
Betty's school bag. "What's the trouble this
morning?" she asked.

"Greatest common divisor and interest,"
Betty replied, promptly.

"Why, they're not one bit puzzling," Gladys
exclaimed. With Betty's help she laid her
flowers in a row on top of the gate, opened
Betty's arithmetic, and began figuring with
pencil and pad. The two heads, Betty's brown
and Gladys's golden one, bent over the work.

"It's as easy as anything, Betty; just this
way, and so!" Betty's worried frown smoothed
itself into a look of relief and understanding.
She closed the arithmetic with a bang and
flung it back into the bag. "You are such a
comfort, Glad!" she exclaimed, as she pinned
on her nosegay and started away. "I'll stop
on my way home this afternoon and bring you
to-morrow's lessons. There's Pegeen coming,"
she added, a bit scornfully.

Gladys watched with what seemed a little
anxiety the slow approach of Pegeen. Her
auburn hair, cut short, was untidy. Her step

was slow and heavy, and she kept her eyes on the ground as she came. She might have passed without stopping if Gladys had not reached out her arms, crying,

"Pegeen! O, wait a minute, please!"

Pegeen stopped and looked up. Instinctively she put her hand over the ugly tear in her brown serge skirt. Pegeen's mother was so busy washing for the whole town that she seemed never to have time for keeping her own big brood tidy. Pegeen herself, at twelve, was the eldest of the family and spent her time out of school tending the younger ones and ironing the plain clothes. Pegeen was proud, with all the pride of generations of fine Irish ancestors, and she knew that the girls in school looked down upon her, thought her slatternly, and left her out of their fun.

But no one could resist Gladys' sunshine smile.

"O, Pegeen, I was waiting for you. I've got such a surprise for you!" At her words Pegeen's freckled face crinkled itself into the merriest kind of laughter. She was pretty with an elfish, eery kind of charm. Every line of her shabby little figure expressed a joyful eagerness as Gladys twisted herself around and pulled a parcel from the back of her wheeled chair.

"I hope it will fit," she said, anxiously, as she unfolded her surprise. "Mother helped me to make it, and we cut it from an eleven-year-old pattern because you're so small for your age. Isn't it lovely, Pegeen? Not another girl in our class has such a pretty one!"

Glad· ، held up a pale yellow linen smock, embroidered in cross stitch with soft green shamrock leaves. A border of these outlined the round neck, there was a bunch of the leaves on each pocket and at the wrists, and even the hem had a trailing line of shamrock that looked as if the leaves had been freshly picked from the moist earth and laid there to decorate the forlorn little Irish maid.

"You can put it right on over your waist, Pegeen," Gladys said, "and it is going to cover up all the worn spots in your skirt and look lovely with the brown. It's early; run in our sitting room and mother will help you put it on."

Pegeen folded the smock in her arms and went up the path to the house. When she came back to Gladys she was quite transformed. The smock fitted perfectly and brought out the bright lights of her hair and her hazel eyes. A brown ribbon tied back her smoothed locks and her face was aglow with happiness.

"I'll look like the other girls now, Glad,"

she said. "I'll be making some of these smocks myself too if you'll help me. Thank you!" she threw her arms around Gladys's neck.

"I will. Run along to school now, Pegeen," Gladys said. Then another thought flashed into her mind and she put it into words: "Don't tell the girls that I made you smock, Pegeen, if you'd rather not."

Pegeen's eyes flashed. "I'll be telling the girls the first minute I see them," she said. "It'll make them love me to know that you love me," she added softly as she went on to school.

Until the last bell rang Gladys was a queen reviewing the loving ranks of her subjects as her classmates went by to school. Her bright smile brought answering smiles to the faces of two who had been quarreling. She helped one with a difficult bit of French translation; another with the bead work she was doing for her Camp Fire dress. So it was every pleasant day, and when it stormed the girls could wave to Gladys as she sat and watched for them in her front window. She was their sun and their rainbow.

The warmer days and the close of school were hard, though, for Gladys. The doctor was positive that she would walk by fall, but she had always been the leader of the girls' vacation fun and it hurt her to be no longer a part of it all. She had only occasional glimpses of the girls, and when she did see them they were mysteriously whispering over some secret plan.

"I suppose it's about their Fourth of July picnic, mother," she said the day before the Fourth. "But I thought they would tell me about it." Quick tears filled her eyes.

Her mother put her hands on the little invalid's cheeks and lifted the sorrowful little face toward hers.

"I know just how hard it is to be left out," she said, "but this is the first Fourth of July, Glad, in all your life that you've had a chance to really be a soldier. Be brave, little girl, and to-morrow you shall wear the colors, your red linen skirt, a white middy, and a new blue hair ribbon—red because you will be brave, white for your goodness all this long shut-in time, and blue for having been so true to your friends."

Gladys clapped her hands.

"I will be a soldier," she cried. "I shall really celebrate Fourth of July!"

Dressed for the day, Gladys wheeled her chair out into the center of the garden the shining afternoon of the Fourth. The garden itself seemed to be keeping the holiday. The red rambler still flung its trailing splendor over the bower at the gateway, the corn-flowers made bright blue fields here and there, and the white verbena and sweet alyssum lay in stars between. Up and down the street Gladys could see the glorious folds of the Stars and Stripes and she heard an occasional drum beat or the flare of a trumpet.

She had hardly settled herself and begun to feel the spirit of the day when her eyes were caught and held by a procession winding its way down the street. She leaned forward to see better; then her eyes shone with excitement.

"The girls are on their way to the picnic," she thought, "and they are coming down this way so that I can see them. There's Pegeen leading, with a big flag. Wasn't it nice of the girls to choose her to carry the flag? And there's Betty next with such a big basket! Nearly all the girls have packages. I guess they are planning for a lot of supper. I hope they won't go by without stopping, although I can't expect them to think of me when they are on their way to their Fourth of July picnic."

The thoughts raced through Gladys's mind, and before she had time to wheel herself to the gate the Fourth of July picnic procession had reached it. The girls stopped, turned—

they were streaming in the gate! Dressed in white with red or blue ribbons, the girls surrounded Gladys's chair while Pegeen knelt at her feet and spread the Stars and Stripes over her.

"We were so afraid that you would find out, Glad," Betty said. "Your mother didn't tell you, did she?"

"We are going to have you for the Goddess of Liberty," Pegeen said.

"And have our Fourth of July picnic here," the other girls explained as they opened baskets and bundles and began the work of transforming the garden into a bit of fairyland.

Soon red and blue lanterns hung from the piazza and the trees. Folds of bunting were festooned from shrub to shrub, and a cloth of the same was laid over the rustic table. The picnic baskets emptied themselves of tongue and ham sandwiches, tied with narrow blue ribbon, glasses of red currant jelly and little round frosted cakes, each with a tiny American flag stuck in the top. Gladys's mother brought out a big glass bowl of lemonade, in which floated crimson cherries, and a box of make-believe cannon firecrackers, each full of red and white peppermint drops.

It was surprising how many games the girls had planned that Gladys was able to play.

She was their leader in Hide the Flag, which they played in a circle like Button, Button, in Simon Says Thumbs Up, Charades, Twenty Questions, and Forfeits. Betty went in the house and played the piano so that they could hear it through the open window and sing "America" and the "Star-Spangled Banner." Then Gladys, still wrapped in the flag, sat at the head of the table as they ate their picnic supper.

"It has been the best Fourth of July I ever had," Gladys said happily, as they all sat quietly in the early dusk, watching an occasional skyrocket burst over the town and the twinkling red and blue lights of the lanterns that shone in the garden.

"Ours too!" Betty said.

"Because we spent it with you," Pegeen added. "We all think you're so brave, and good, and true to us, Glad."

Gladys started, remembering her mother's words. Then she stretched out her hands to the girls.

"O, I do thank you so much," she said, "for helping with my red, white, and blue day!"

MERCURY'S BRAVE FLIGHT

JANET read again, for countless times, the letter from Marjory, the daughter of the quarter-master sergeant of Fort Hope.

DEAR JANET:

Tuesday will be your birthday, and mine too. Won't you come over here and spend the day with me? We will have a birthday party, all by ourselves. Do say that you will come.

Lovingly,

MARJORY WAYNE.

Of course she was going. Looking about the big, bare living room of the ranch that was her home, Janet remembered Marjory's more comfortable quarters in the barracks over at the Fort. Quarter-master Wayne had only recently been assigned to this far away post on the plains. Bright rugs, and hangings, pictures, books, and dolls to sew for! Of these luxuries Janet had enjoyed a glimpse when she had visited Marjory for the first time. Marjory herself seemed to Janet, little plains girl that she was, almost a doll too. She had lived in a city all her twelve years. Her yellow hair floated in a bright cloud over her shoulders. Her dainty gingham dresses and gay linen smocks and ribbons seemed very wonderful to Janet, who had worn khaki and buckskin ever since she could remember. And Marjory was as merry and sweet-tempered as she was dainty and lovable.

"O, mother!" Janet sighed happily. "This is Tuesday, and it is my birthday, and I am going over to the Fort."

"Have you a gift for Marjory?" her mother asked, looking out of the window and across the wide sweep of the plains that separated the ranch from Fort Hope.

"O, yes, mother, and I know she will love it," Janet said, running over to the chest of drawers and pulling out a necklace of big, bright Indian beads. It was a gift to make any little girl's heart glad, strung of beads as many colored as a rainbow.

"I have another present for Marjory too," Janet said, "a new bridle."

At the last word her mother turned quickly and looked at her. "You will ride Mercury over?"

"Yes, mother."

Janet looked up questioningly as her mother crossed the room and put both her hands on the little girl's shoulders.

"Do you think you could bear to be parted from Mercury? Could you leave him at the Fort?" she asked, a little falteringly.

"Leave Mercury at the Fort?" Janet repeated her mother's words in wonder. "Leave my pony?"

Her mother explained, looking tenderly into the little girl's wide opened brown eyes.

"You know, dear child, how bad a season it has been for the ranch. There was the scourge among the cattle and the pasturage was poor for the sheep. They want horses badly at the Fort to ship south at once, and especially ponies. Mercury is the best and the swiftest pony on the ranch, and the government will pay father a good sum for him. I am so sorry, Janet, since you have been riding him so long and love him so much."

Quick tears rose to Janet's eyes, and she could not speak because of a cruel choking in her throat. Sell Mercury, the fleet little brown ranch bronco who had carried her to and from school, and for long rides across the prairie as long as she could remember? It seemed to Janet that she could not bear it. All the joy of the birthday party was gone now. But when she looked up into her mother's face Janet knew that her sorrow was as great over selling Mercury as was her own. Janet bravely kept back her tears, throwing her arms around her mother.

"It's all right. I'll start now so as to go by

way of the ford and have my last ride on Mercury a long one. I'll leave him at the Fort and come back on the stage this afternoon." Janet was smiling now, but her smile was like an April sun, dimmed by the mist of a shower.

As she mounted Mercury the tough little brown pony turned his head for the lump of sugar that Janet always carried for him in the pocket of her riding skirt. His long, dusky mane brushed her cheek as she put her head down close to it to hide another quick flow of tears. Then they were off, keeping pace with the wind over the wide expanse of plain.

Janet hugged close to the pony's shaggy sides, feeling comfort in the touch of his warm, brown coat. She fancied that he had, in some unknown way, sensed the approaching separation, for he trotted instead of galloping, almost stopping at Janet's favorite haunts of dell and sparse woods. There were a few late prairie blossoms to be seen, here and there. The air was chilly, but sweet with the odors of the grasses that the wind brought. In places the riding was hard, for the late fall rains had gouged out the trail and left treacherous bogs and pitfalls.

Mercury did not make one misstep though.

As he trotted along, head up and long mane flying like a cloud in the wind, Janet leaned over, putting her head close to his and speaking to him as if he were able to understand her.

"It's our last ride together, Mercury; do you know it? O, it doesn't seem as if I could bear it, but I mustn't let mother and father know. I hope your new master will be kind to you, little pony-boy. I think I'll write a letter to him, whoever he is, and tell him that you need love just as much as you need oats. I shall think I hear your little hoofs beating in my dreams at night. O, Mercury, I don't want any pony in the world but you." Janet's tears blurred her eyes. It was only because the wind brought her a far away cry, "Help!" that she straightened in her saddle and turned Mercury in the direction of the sound.

She touched the pony ever so lightly with one spurred boot. He was off on the instant as Janet guided him in the direction of the ravine. The road became steep now, slanting toward this cut in the plains where low hills on either side shut in a swift little stream; and the trail was rough with broken boulders and rain-soaked earth.

Half way down the ravine Janet heard the cries more plainly.

"Help! Help!"

"Hurry, Mercury! We must make haste. Be careful; it's steep here, and if you lose your footing we'll both fall and no one can help us," Janet urged in the pony's ear, caressing him as much with her voice as with her hands. He responded, picking his way almost as skillfully as an antelope on the steep descent. Now they were almost down, and Janet saw the source of the cries of distress.

The mail team, a lumbering old stage that had been pressed into the government's service, had been on its way to the Fort with its precious bags of letters and papers. The stream, swollen by the rains, had softened the clay banks and overflowed them as well. In attempting to cross the ford the heavy team had stuck in the mud. The driver was helpless. His pair of horses floundered in the water and mud. But the flow of the angry little stream threatened any moment to displace the wheels of the team, overturn it, and dash driver and horses down in its turbid flow.

"Why don't you go on my horse to the Fort for help?" Janet called.

"I can't. I must stay with the mail bags; I'm not allowed to leave them," the man called back. "If I had another pair of horses, I could pull out. As it is I don't know how long I shall be able to stand this," he said, despairingly.

"I'm going to the Fort; I'll get help for you," Janet said.

The man tried to smile. "It will be too late," he said, "if you go around the ravine, for the horses can't stand this much longer. The only chance would be if you could cross by the ford. That takes half the time, but it would be too much for a girl and a pony."

"I'll ford it," Janet called back as she tightened her hold of the reins and Mercury plunged into the water.

At best it was a dangerous ford, uneven all the way. Here the slippery stones would give way their precarious footing to deep places where a horse must swim, buffeted by the current. There his hoofs would stick fast, glued to the clay-bottom of the stream. Now, with the stream swollen to twice its natural width, the difficulties were doubled.

Janet clasped Mercury tightly around his neck. He shivered, trembled a little as the water touched his haunches, but he heard the coaxing voice in his ear.

"Don't fail me, Mercury. Good little horse, be brave and don't let the river get the best of you. I'll hold as fast as I can, but you must take care of me, for you're going to be a little army pony, and that's the bravest kind of a horse in the world. Don't fail the United States now, Mercury!"

If the pony could not interpret Janet's words, at least he recognized the pleading tones and he felt the urge of the little clinging body on his back. When he lost his footing on the slimy stones, he found it again. When he stepped off into deep water, he was a shaggy little sea horse swimming valiantly along with his foaming nostrils and red eye balls well out of the water. At the steep ascent of the opposite bank, his feet buried themselves in the mire. He wavered, his knees bent ever so little as if he were going to fall, but he heard, again, the coaxing voice in his ear.

"Good little Mercury. Don't give up now, so near the end! Play we're carrying Old Glory with us to the Fort. That's it; now we're up the bank and it's all a straight stretch now to the finish. But go as fast as the wind, little horse."

Mercury did not need spurs. Foaming, caked with mud, and shivering he scrambled up the bank. He did not pause an instant. He raced with the wind. It was only a short time until the white buildings of the Fort were in sight, and Janet, soaked, muddy, and almost crying, reached the end of the barracks where Marjory waited for her.

It was growing dusk, and candles for the birthday party were lighted. The open door, welcoming the drenched, muddy little figure in khaki, almost dazed her with the beauty it disclosed: growing plants and a table gleaming with dainty dishes and silver; a huge pink birthday cake in the center, and Marjory in white with pink ribbons to greet her. It was small wonder that the guests looked in surprise at Janet, standing outside beside her plucky little steed.

"The mail team's stuck in the ravine. The man needs help or the horses will go down with the current. He said an extra pair would be enough to pull him out. He said you must hurry." Janet's words came clearly and fast.

The quarter-master sergeant was beside her now, after having given quick orders for the immediate starting of a relief party.

"I don't understand. How did you know?" he asked.

"I heard him calling and I went down in the ravine. He said there wasn't much time, but I came across the ford," Janet explained.

"You are a very brave little girl," the officer said, taking Janet's hand. Then he put his hand on Mercury's wet side. "A fine horse too."

"Yes, sir," Janet said, looking up bravely as she slipped Mercury's halter into the quartermaster's hand. "I brought him to you. He's my horse, but father says you need horses in the army and we've had a poor season on the ranch. He's the best little pony that ever lived," she finished with a catch in her voice.

Dry, and dressed in one of Marjory's dainty dresses, Janet tried to enjoy the party. Her bridle for Marjory had been washed downstream, but the necklace which she had hung around her neck was safe. It delighted Marjory more than any of her other gifts. Marjory's gift to Janet was a doll that would be a little sister to Janet during the lonely winter days on the ranch. But as Janet stroked its long brown hair she was reminded of the feeling of Mercury's soft mane. A doll would be a comfort, she knew, but how she would miss Mercury!

She was a little surprised that Marjory did not urge her to stay longer when she suggested going home early. Marjory's eyes almost sparkled as she helped Janet to put on her dried riding clothes.

"I'll just be able to catch the stage," Janet said.

"O, I don't think you are to ride home in

the stage, Janet," Marjory said, mysteriously, as she led Janet to the door.

There stood Mercury, dry, brushed, fed, ready to go home.

"Mercury!" Janet ran to the pony and laid her hands on his bent head. "I don't understand," she said, turning to the quartermaster, who had come out with his little daughter to say good-by.

"A birthday gift from Uncle Sam to a brave little girl," the officer explained. "We will buy some of your father's other horses at a price that will allow of your keeping this one. We want him within easy distance of the Fort and you to ride him again some time as you did to-day in the service of the government."

"O, Mercury, it wasn't our last ride!" Janet said, joyously, as she jumped on the pony's back and started home with her doll under her arm.